———*The*———

COMPLETE
WORSHIP
LEADER

The
COMPLETE WORSHIP LEADER

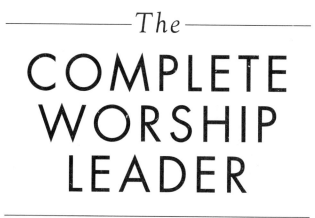

KEVIN J. NAVARRO

Baker Books

A Division of Baker Book House Co
Grand Rapids, Michigan 49516

© 2001 by Kevin J. Navarro

Published by Baker Books
a division of Baker Book House Company
P.O. Box 6287, Grand Rapids, MI 49516-6287

Printed in the United States of America

Library of Congress Cataloging-in-Publication Data

Navarro, Kevin J.
    The complete worship leader / Kevin J. Navarro.
        p.   cm.
    Includes bibliographical references and index.
    ISBN 0-8010-9116-0 (paper)
    1. Public worship. I. Title.
    BV15 .N38 2001
    264—dc21   2001037528

For current information about all releases from Baker Book House, visit our web site:
http://www.bakerbooks.com

CONTENTS

FOREWORD

THE WORSHIP LEADER ROLE as we know it is two decades old at best. For most of that time, there have been no worship leader training centers, no worship leading degrees, and few seasoned mentors. It's been a rough and unpredictable journey, let's face it! Oh, there have been valuable lessons, to be sure. Yet, if we're honest, many of us wish that we'd not learned so many of those lessons after the fact; if we would have had more solid preparation, perhaps we wouldn't have spent the first decade in that circular hamster contraption called "What Not to Do!"

It used to be that there were pastors and there were music directors. Either there was already a liturgy in place or the pastor planned the shape of the service. Whichever situation music directors found themselves in, they knew their territory, and it definitely did not include a degree in theology. It was the pastor's job to make sure the service was about honoring God (hopefully the RIGHT God). It was the pastor's job to make sure the gospel was proclaimed. It was the pastor's job to insert prayers, Scripture readings, and announcements appropriate for the day. Neither did a music director's territory include a degree in the arts. Two decades ago, music directors were not expected to know a whit about drama, painting, poetry, or dance. Their job was one-dimensional: Find music to match the Scripture for the day or the pastor's message, then prepare the most excellent, thematically congruent package of prelude, liturgical responses, hymns, choral anthem, solo, and postlude possible.

Well, guess what? In the last two decades, several developments have made the old role of worship director obsolete. One, congregations are for the most part theologically illiterate. We can't assume they know what worship is, nor can we assume they know the basics of creation, fall, and redemption.

Two, people's authenticity meters are becoming more sophisticated and finer tuned with each passing Sunday. It's as if people are handed night-vision glasses when they come in the door. They can spot counterfeit faith in a nanosecond.

Three, we've finally figured out that worship does not equal music. It may include music, but the two are not synonymous. Which brings us to the fourth and final development: In the new millennium, people come to church first and foremost to experience God, not to get an information download. And they are going to want to use all of their senses—not just their ears—in the God-encounter they expect to happen. Whether we like it or not, ours is an increasingly mystical, multisensory, right-brained world. Music on "cruise control," music as perfunctory preparation to a cerebral, three-point sermon is just not going to cut it.

As I read Kevin Navarro's manuscript, I found myself whispering, "Of course!" This all makes sense. To be an effective worship leader in this new day means becoming "complete." It means more than having a prestigious music degree, more than playing incredible guitar riffs, more than being "The Voice." It is to be theologically awake and responsible; to be daily maturing in faith and practice (i.e., authentic); to be conversant with diverse, artistic expressions (the difference between working with eight Crayolas and a box of sixty-four); and to be able to lead others into passionate, Christ-honoring expressions of their gifts. Fellow worship leaders, if becoming a complete worship leader were Mission Impossible, God would not have called us to it. God would not have placed us where we are—in this congregation, this community, this century, this millennium, now. But God has. And in doing so, God calls us to a supreme walk of faith and intentionality. May this much-needed book, *The Complete Worship Leader*, serve as your ready guide for a most exciting journey. Thank you, Kevin.

SALLY MORGENTHALER

ACKNOWLEDGMENTS

I WOULD LIKE TO THANK Robb Redman for encouraging me to write this book and for being my theological mentor during my studies at Fuller Seminary. I would also like to thank Robert N. Hosack and the editorial staff at Baker Books for making this book possible.

I would like to thank everyone who personally guided me in the ministry of writing: Dallas Willard, C. Peter Wagner, Sally Morganthaler, Phillis Klein, Ken Gire, Reg Grant, and Calvin Miller.

A special thanks to my teachers and mentors: Alan Combs, Alan Eberhardt, Bill Pfund, Cam Floria, Chris and Carole Beatty, Harold Westing, Vernon Grounds, Craig Blomberg, Scott Martin, Bob Wilbraham, Dick Patty, Dallas Willard, Darrel Johnson, and Earl Palmer.

To Pastor John and the Bethany family: I am so fortunate to have a wonderful church. Thanks for your encouragement to me as a pastor and worship leader. Thanks for your prayer support. A special thanks to David and Mary Sue Ong for their interest in this project and for their constant encouragement.

To my family: Susan, Timothy, Matthew, Joshua, and Aaron. I am so blessed to have a wonderful wife and healthy kids. You are so much fun to be with. To my parents who have always encouraged and supported me: Ruben D. and Velma Navarro.

Thanks to those who had a part in leading me to Christ: Alan Combs, Todd Williams, and the Calvary Chapel family. Most importantly, I would like to thank the Lord Jesus Christ for having mercy on me, a sinner.

INTRODUCTION

THE WORSHIP SERVICE is the most important event in the local church, and the engine that drives all programming. Church health depends on what happens in that experience. If the worship service is deteriorating, growth in other ministries will be temporal and marginal. When all is said and done, dynamic worship services produce dynamic churches.

Yet, dynamic worship is not merely a church growth factor. Worship is the reason for the existence of the church. "But you are a chosen people, a royal priesthood, a holy nation, a people belonging to God, that you may declare the praises of him who called you out of darkness into his wonderful light. Once you were not a people, but now you are the people of God; once you had not received mercy, but now you have received mercy" (1 Peter 2:9–10).[1] Evangelism is "gossiping the gospel" to our family, friends, and neighbors. This boasting in the Lord is what worship is all about. We declare through the arts, symbol, and language what the Lord has done for us. Some people say that we should praise God for who he is, not because of what he can do for us. But this is an unfortunate distinction. We only know who God is because of what he has created and redeemed, in essence, what he has done. With this consideration, the local church is one of the best places for evangelism. This is where we proclaim Jesus Christ as the King of kings and the Lord of lords.[2]

For this important event to succeed, we need dynamic leadership. The purpose of this book is to describe the process of *becoming* a complete worship leader; the participle is intentional. Worship leading is a process in that we are always discovering the God who has revealed himself and what he has to say about worship. We are always trying to figure out how to engage the people of God in active participation.

In the phrase *a complete worship leader*, I am referring to the congruity that is required in worship leading. This consists of four elements: theology, discipleship, artistry, and leadership. Effective worship leading brings together these elements. The worship leader who does not possess attributes from these four categories is at best impaired. The major sections of this work will focus on becoming a theologian, a disciple, an artist, and a leader. By mastering these four categories, the ordinary worship leader will become a complete worship leader.

Within these categories there will be two chapters that summarize these sections. In part one (becoming a theologian) we will look at revelation and redemption. In part two (becoming a disciple) we will look at salvation and proclamation. In part three (becoming an artist) we will look at appreciation and creation. In the last section (becoming a leader) we will look at demonstration and participation. Two additional chapters pertaining to leadership conclude this work.

This book is based on research and a personal journey. I write as one who leads worship in the local church. I have learned what to avoid in worship leading. Equally important, I have discovered principles that enrich worship leadership. May this work influence our worship in the body of Christ. May it be used by God, in a practical way, to help senior pastors, worship leaders, and others with the most important event that will happen in their churches this week.

BECOMING
A THEOLOGIAN

INTRODUCTION
TO PART ONE

EVERY WORSHIP LEADER must become a theologian. Theology is important because it deals with our ideas about God. It makes a difference how we worship God. William H. Willimon, in his book *Worship As Pastoral Care* states:

> To ask the theological question is simply to ask, What does our worship say about God? or the corollary, What does God say to us about our worship? Surely this is the toughest and most basic question to be asked, but, curiously, it is often the last question we ask. If we think about our worship at all, usually we think in terms of, What do *I* want from our worship? or, What do *my people* want from our worship? without daring to be so bold as to ask, What does God want from our worship? Is our worship the worship of the God of Abraham, Isaac, and Jacob; or is it the worship of Baal, Aphrodite, and Cupid? Does our worship have integrity when measured by the biblical standards for what our prayer and praise should be? So much of our worship is self-centered, mundane, and tame.

How are we to be faithful to the gospel; how do we know the difference between secular idolatry and Christian liturgy unless we ask, and in some measure answer, the theological question?[1]

One of my professors, Dallas Willard, said in a lecture that "we live at the mercy of our ideas." This is especially true when it comes to our ideas about God and worship. Our theology must be accurate if our worship is to be accurate. An intentional neglect of the God who has revealed himself will degenerate into idolatry. The premise, worship is not initiated by us, will begin this discussion of becoming a theologian. God initiates worship, not us. God has revealed himself through what has been classified by theologians as general revelation and special revelation. When I speak of special revelation from this point on, I will refer to it as redemption.

General revelation refers to the knowledge that we have as the result of God creating the cosmos and the moral conscience within each human being. The term *general revelation* is used in that by very nature of living in this world, all will experience this whether believer or not. This is the starting point for a theology of worship.

In chapter one, I will address not only general revelation but also the topic of idolatry. Every human being is a worshiper. The question is not *are* we worshiping but *what* are we worshiping? Romans 1 addresses the issue of idolatry as fundamentally an issue of rebellion.

In the second chapter, I will address the topic of redemption. In that the unregenerate human being fails to worship God and in that God holds us accountable for our idolatry, we must be born again if we desire to worship the living God. For the nation of Israel, the exodus was essential to worship. For the Christian, the death and resurrection of Christ are essential to worship. As the apostle Paul states in 1 Corinthians 15:17, "if Christ has not been raised, your faith is futile; you are still in your sins."[2] Therefore, true worship is only possible for those who have been redeemed by the blood of the Lamb.

---
one

REVELATION

"BY FAITH WE UNDERSTAND that the universe was formed at God's command, so that what is seen was not made out of what was visible" (Heb. 11:3). Worship is initiated by the God who has revealed himself. The psalmist says, "The heavens declare the glory of God; the skies proclaim the work of his hands. Day after day they pour forth speech; night after night they display knowledge. There is no speech or language where their voice is not heard. Their voice goes out into all the earth, their words to the ends of the world" (Ps. 19:1–4).

Becoming a complete worship leader begins with appreciating the God of creation. It is this God who creates that gives us inspiration for our own creativity. It is the God of the cosmos who prompts us to worship.

Many churches have altogether lost the mystery in worship. And the problem does not lie with God being overly familiar to us. Some people would make the argument that the more familiar we are with something, the more likely we are to be bored. This is not true. When we look at a rose and inhale its wonderful scent, are we not amazed? So it should be with our relationship with God. The more we know of God, the more astonished we are with his love. The problem with modern Christianity is not familiarity with God but ignorance, unresponsiveness, and apathy.[1]

When we look at the leaves bursting forth from a silver maple, the Creator is trying to get our attention. Our pathetic blindness restrains us from seeing God. Worship begins by encountering the God who is there. This is known as general revelation, because whether one is a believer or not, every human being by nature of living in this world receives the goods.[2] In his book *Engaging with God*, David Peterson states, "Acceptable worship does not start with human intuition or inventiveness, but with the action of God."[3] Our understanding of this truth is imperative if we are to rightly understand the topic of worship.

God said, "You shall have no other gods before me. You shall not make for yourself an idol in the form of anything in heaven above or on the earth beneath or in the waters below" (Exod. 20:3–4).[4] There was to be a clear distinction between the gods made with human hands and the Lord God Almighty. God's people would know the difference by paying attention to what God revealed about himself. The only way they could worship in spirit and in truth was to know the One whom they were seeking to worship.

Theology is about discovery, not invention. We do not make up a god; we discover the God who is there. J. I. Packer has stated that "theology is for doxology and devotion."[5]

It is vital that we become childlike, engaging all our senses to appreciate the Creator. "You alone are the LORD. You made the heavens, even the highest heavens, and all their starry host, the earth and all that is on it, the seas and all that is in them. You give life to everything, and the multitudes of heaven worship you" (Neh. 9:6). Having eyes to see God's creation is needed to become a complete worship leader.

Poets are often inspired by nature. One of my favorite poems is *Polishing the Petoskey Stone* by Luci Shaw. In it, she describes a Petoskey stone, which, after being rubbed with the hands, begins to take on the appearance of an eyeball. It takes a careful eye to spot one of these stones on the beaches of Michigan. Initially, it looks like any other rock with all of the dirt and muck. But once you begin to polish it, you will notice a translucent appearance, one of looking into the eyes of a soul.[6]

As I think of this poem, I am reminded of the way God has revealed himself through his creation. He has created the galaxies, stars, planets, skies, earth, water, and every living organism with the skill of a detailed artist. He has done all of this to reveal himself. God wants us to know that he exists and that he is a God of order and beauty.

In the New Testament, when Paul and Barnabas were in Lystra, the people began to worship them following the healing of the man who was crippled. They called Barnabas Zeus, and they called Paul Hermes, because he was the chief speaker. The text tells us, "But when the apostles Barnabas and Paul heard of this, they tore their clothes and rushed out into the crowd, shouting: 'Men, why are you doing this? We too are only men, human like you. We are bringing you good news, telling you to turn from these worthless things to the living God, who made heaven and earth and sea and everything in them'" (Acts 14:14–15). Notice that Paul and Barnabas offer the corrective by directing attention to the Creator, not to themselves. We must deal with the fact that there is a God who has created the heavens and the earth. He is Sovereign over history and the natural order.[7] The inception of worship is to acknowledge this God who created the universe. From the farthest star to the intricacies of the biological world, there is a Master Designer behind it all. Part of our own creative design is that we long to be worshipers of the One who made the universe. May we ascribe to the Lord the glory and honor due his name.[8]

THE RELATIONSHIP BETWEEN CREATION AND THE SABBATH

I find it fascinating that the Sabbath is linked to the creation. "For in six days the LORD made the heavens and the earth, the sea, and all that is in them, but he rested on the seventh day. Therefore the LORD blessed the Sabbath day and made it holy" (Exod. 20:11). Rabbi Abraham Joshua Heschel offers the most profound insight in his book *The Sabbath:*

> It is, indeed, a unique occasion at which the distinguished word *qadosh* is used for the first time: in the book of Genesis at the end of the story of creation. How extremely significant is the fact that it is applied to time: "And God blessed the seventh *day* and made it *holy.*" There is no reference in the record of creation to any object in space that would be endowed with the quality of holiness. This is a radical departure from accustomed religious thinking. The mythical mind would expect that, after heaven and earth have been established, God would create a holy place—a holy mountain or a holy spring—whereupon a sanctuary is to be established. Yet it seems as if to the Bible it is *holiness in time,* the Sabbath, which comes first.[9]

This holiness of time, which the covenant people were to observe, is linked to God's creating for six days and then resting on the seventh. God wants to be acknowledged on the Sabbath as the One who created and rested. He wants to have a day set aside that would remind his people of how he alone is the Creator. The complete worship leader must appreciate the God of creation; it is from this starting point that he or she will have equilibrium.

General Revelation in the Moral Conscience of Every Human Being

The next element of general revelation is that God created every human being in the image of himself. "Then God said, Let us make man in our image, in our likeness, and let them rule over the fish of the sea and the birds of the air, over the livestock, over all the earth, and over all the creatures that move along the ground. So God created man in his own image, in the image of God he created him; male and female he created them" (Gen. 1:26–27).[10] We have dignity in that we reflect this God of the universe.

Every Monday morning, I have breakfast with my oldest son, Timothy. We have recently been studying how we have been created in God's image. My seven-year-old can articulate the unlikeliness that his dog or goldfish will ask him to play a game of checkers. The ability to use language is one of the clearest indications that we reflect God's glory differently than the rest of the animal kingdom. But this is not all.

God created us with a moral conscience. Consequently, we are without excuse when it comes to the knowledge of God. Every human being is responsible for this knowledge. Part of general revelation is that each of us has been created with a moral compass. We know right and wrong. It is because we do have this moral quality that God holds us accountable.

Idolatry: A Human Predisposition

Every human being is a worshiper. The Bible tells us that if we do not worship the Creator, we will worship the creation. Our hearts will move from a vertical posture to a horizontal posture. We will embrace naturalism instead of

23

theism. The apostle Paul said, "The wrath of God is being revealed from heaven against all the godlessness and wickedness of men who suppress the truth by their wickedness, since what may be known about God is plain to them, because God has made it plain to them. For since the creation of the world God's invisible qualities—his eternal power and divine nature—have been clearly seen, being understood from what has been made, so that men are without excuse" (Rom. 1:18–20).

Idolatry is humankind's intentional neglect of the God who has revealed himself. When we look at God's creation, our response should be to give him thanks. We enjoy the gift of life, his provision, and countless other blessings on a daily basis.

Worship begins with the realization that without God, there is no life, no help for the basic necessities of life; we recognize our poverty and his provision. We need to tell God how much we appreciate him. This is the inception of worship, the starting point of doxology. Without a healthy view of the Creator, our worship will always be handicapped.

Since God has initiated worship, one might think that our inclination would be to worship this God. Yet history tells us that the opposite is true. Our natural impulse is to worship everything *but* God. We are idol factories. Why is this?

Why Are We Inclined toward Idolatry?

The primary reason that we are inclined toward idolatry is because we have inherited a depraved nature. Because of this depravity, we love everything but God. The apostle Paul states in 1 Corinthians 15:22 that "in Adam all die." Paul addresses this subject of Adam being a representative in Romans 5:12–21:

Therefore, just as sin entered the world through one man, and death through sin, and in this way death came to all men, because all sinned—for before the law was given, sin was in the world. But sin is not taken into account when there is no law. Nevertheless, death reigned from the time of Adam to the time of Moses, even over those who did not sin by breaking a command, as did Adam, who was a pattern of the one to come.

But the gift is not like the trespass. For if the many died by the trespass of the one man, how much more did God's grace and the gift that came by the grace of the one man, Jesus Christ, overflow to the many! Again, the gift of God is not like the result of the one man's sin: The judgment followed one sin and brought condemnation, but the gift followed many trespasses and brought justification. For if, by the trespass of the one man, death reigned through that one man, how much more will those who receive God's abundant provision of grace and of the gift of righteousness reign in life through the one man, Jesus Christ.

Consequently, just as the result of one trespass was con-demnation for all men, so also the result of one act of right-eousness was justification that brings life for all men. For just as through the disobedience of the one man the many were made sinners, so also through the obedience of the one man the many will be made righteous.

The law was added so that the trespass might increase. But where sin increased, grace increased all the more, so that, just as sin reigned in death, so also grace might reign through righteousness to bring eternal life through Jesus Christ our Lord.

In this passage, the apostle Paul compares Adam and Jesus Christ: Both are representatives. In the same way that condemnation is imputed to us the moment we are born physically, the righteousness of Christ is imputed to us when we are born again. This is why Jesus told Nicodemus that he needed to be born again if he wanted to see the King-dom of God (John 3). If we are only physically born, we will face condemnation. We are not sinners because we sin; we sin because we are sinners. It is our nature to sin. It is our nature to worship other gods. As Paul states in the Book of Romans, we are without excuse. We are rebels and enemies of God.

We worship what we love. This is why being born again is so necessary. It is not just an issue of eternal salvation but an issue of worship. The unregenerate do not desire God, do not love God, and do not worship God. We must keep this in mind when developing a theology of worship for "seekers."

When I say that unbelievers do not worship God, I am not saying believers shouldn't show hospitality. We must reach out to the unchurched with the kind of mercy that has been extended to us. We must always have room in our churches for the lost. Jesus said, "It is not the healthy who need a doctor, but the sick. But go and learn what this means: I desire mercy, not sacrifice. For I have not come to call the righteous, but sinners" (Matt. 9:12–13). But remember that only an invasion of the Holy Spirit will liberate these enemy-held hostages.

Repentance—Essential to True Worship

When I was in fifth grade, I begged my parents to buy me a trumpet. They finally agreed and made the purchase at a pawn shop. I used a cleaning rag to shine my trumpet every day. This instrument had the most fantastic shine. If I had had some car wax, I would have used that too. But it wasn't until I started taking trumpet lessons two years later that I learned I needed to clean the *inside* of the trumpet. I'll never forget discovering a putrid-smelling green slime residing within my shiny brass instrument. It was a horrifying experience.

In a similar way this is what goes on in our lives. To the outside world, we are shined up; we look great. But on the inside, we are full of smelly garbage. We can go on for years without ever cleaning the inside. 1 John 1:8–10 says, "If we claim to be without sin, we deceive ourselves and the truth is not in us. If we confess our sins, he is faithful and just and will forgive us our sins and purify us from all unrighteousness. If we claim we have not sinned, we make him out to be a liar and his word has no place in our lives." Repentance is fundamental to worship. Graham Kendrick has put it this way: "The genuineness of our worship cannot be measured in decibels of sound, and although it is vital that we express our love for God vocally, he looks to see the evidence in our lives. We do not always think of repentance as worship, but it can be much easier to sing a rousing hymn than to turn away from our favorite sin. A sinful act involves worship of the wrong kind, submitting ourselves at that moment to serve the appetites of our pride or lust, and so repentance is literally a transfer of our worship back to the One who rightfully owns it."[11]

It is incongruent to love God and store up treasure in this world. Jesus said that where our treasure is our heart will be also (Matt. 6:21). We must repent of our love affair with the world. We must put the world behind us and the cross before us. "Do not love the world or anything in the world. If anyone loves the world, the love of the Father is not in him. For everything in the world—the cravings of sinful man, the lust of his eyes and the boasting of what he has and does—comes not from the Father but from the world. The world and its desires pass away, but the man who does the will of God lives forever" (1 John 2:15–17). Why then do those who claim to be Christians fall back into idolatry?

Why Do the Regenerate Slip into Idolatry?

The primary reason those who claim to be born again fall into idolatry is ignorance of the written Word of God. There is an illiteracy today unchallenged in our Christian churches. We do not encourage our people to know the Scriptures. What are we as worship leaders doing about our biblical literacy? Do we know what the Word teaches about God? Have we studied to show ourselves approved?

As worship leaders we can equip ourselves by using a systematic approach to reading the Scriptures, and a one-year Bible is a wonderful place to start. Such a plan usually contains an Old Testament portion, a New Testament portion, a psalm, and a proverb for the day. The whole reading takes about twenty minutes. A plan like this is beneficial because it gives an overview of the Bible and also eliminates the problem of trying to figure out what to read.

Critics say that if we read the Bible in a year we will not meditate on any one portion of Scripture. Certainly I am not advocating a system in which we check off a do-list without understanding the passage. We must always ponder what the Lord is saying to us. I believe we can read the Bible systematically and meditate simultaneously.

When we read the Word, we must read to discover God. Often, however, we tend to read the Bible as a self-help book. We want to learn how we can lead a successful life instead of how we can discover the God who has revealed himself. I recently led a small group Bible study through the Book of Hosea. The group believed the key thought in the book was the unfaithfulness of Israel. I pointed out that the primary thought was not the unfaithfulness of Israel but God's faithfulness and love in the midst of Israel's unfaithfulness. When we read the Bible from this perspective, we will praise God for who he is and what he's done.

If we want to worship God we have to know God. Knowledge comes from being in relationship with God through his Word. He has revealed himself through his creative acts and through his redemptive acts as recorded in the Scriptures. If we are ignorant of these events, we will also be ignorant of the knowledge of God.

We are exhorted in Psalm 46:8–10 to "come and see the works of the LORD, the desolations he has brought on the earth. He makes wars cease to the ends of the earth; he breaks the bow and shatters the spear, he burns the shields with fire. Be still, and know that I am God; I will be exalted among the nations, I will be exalted in the earth." The Lord clearly states that he will be exalted in the earth and that we should strive to be still and know him. This is a desperate need for the complete worship leader. The one who would seek to lead God's people into worship must first know the Lord for himself or herself. We might think that we are worshiping the God of the universe but might only be worshiping the god of our imaginations.

We must repent of our idolatry and come back to a knowledge of the Lord, maker of heaven and earth. We must worship the God who has revealed himself as recorded in creation and through the Scriptures. Worship is not created in a vacuum. Rather, we are recipients of God's goodness and grace, and with appreciative hearts we must respond to God with thanksgiving and praise.

REPRISE

I have said that the complete worship leader must first of all be a theologian and that theology is an issue of revelation. This is the basic material we work with as worship leaders. We must understand that God has revealed himself and that he holds every human being accountable for worship. Furthermore, we have seen that every human being is a worshiper but usually of something other than God. We are therefore condemned to face judgment. As a worship leader, this is fundamental, for it begs the question, "Who is qualified to worship the living God?" This will be the discussion of the next chapter.

two

REDEMPTION

SPECIAL REVELATION STATES that God has revealed himself through his redemptive acts as recorded in the Scriptures.[1] Before we discuss what the New Testament says about God's redemptive acts through Jesus Christ, let us look at the Old Testament, focusing on the exodus. Understanding this event is very important for us because it shaped liturgy for Judaism.

THE GOD WHO REDEEMS HIS PEOPLE

In the Old Testament, the exodus was the climax of worship. It celebrated the deliverance of the nation of Israel from Egyptian bondage. The Book of Exodus records all the details of how the Lord would bring his people into the Promised Land. God wanted to prove to the nations that he was God. We are told in the New Testament that God raised up Pharaoh for this very purpose (Rom. 9:17). He wanted to show his people that he alone could save them from their enemies. He was not a deistic god detached from the world

he created. Rather, he was provident in every event that
took place. This was why the people could rejoice.

One of the first praise songs recorded in our Bible is the
Song of Moses or the Song of Deliverance. This song celebrating how God saved his people is recorded in Exodus 15:

"I will sing to the LORD
For He has triumphed gloriously!
The horse and its rider
He has thrown into the sea!
The LORD is my strength and song,
And He has become my salvation;
He is my God, and I will praise Him.
My father's God, and I will exalt Him.
The LORD is a man of war;
The LORD is His name.
Pharaoh's chariots and his army
    He has cast into the sea;
His chosen captains also
    are drowned in the Red Sea.
The depths have covered them;
They sank to the bottom like a stone.

"Your right hand, O LORD,
    has become glorious in power;
Your right hand, O LORD,
    has dashed the enemy in pieces.
And in the greatness
    of Your excellence
You have overthrown those
    who rose against You;
You sent forth Your wrath
    which consumed them like stubble.
And with the blast of Your nostrils
The waters were gathered together;
The floods stood upright like a heap;
And the depths congealed
    in the heart of the sea.

The enemy said, 'I will pursue,
I will overtake,
I will divide the spoil;
My desire shall be satisfied on them.
I will draw my sword,
My hand shall destroy them,'
You blew with Your wind,
The sea covered them;
They sank like lead
   in the mighty waters.

"Who is like You, O LORD,
   among the gods?
Who is like You, glorious in holiness,
Fearful in praises, doing wonders?
You stretched out Your right hand;
The earth swallowed them.
You in Your mercy have led forth
The people whom You have redeemed;
You have guided them in Your strength
To Your holy habitation.

"The people will hear and be afraid;
Sorrow will take hold of the
   inhabitants of Palestina.
Then the chiefs of Edom
   will be dismayed;
The mighty men of Moab,
Trembling will take hold of them;
All the inhabitants of Canaan
   will melt away.
Fear and dread will fall on them;
By the greatness of Your arm
They will be as still as a stone,
Till Your people pass over, O LORD,
Till the people pass over
Whom You have purchased.
You will bring them in and plant them
In the mountain of Your inheritance,

In the place, O LORD,
    which You have made
For Your own dwelling,
The sanctuary, O LORD,
    which Your hands have established.

"The LORD shall reign forever and ever."

EXODUS 15:1–18 NKJV

This song beautifully describes redemption. It was God who brought his people out of Egypt. It was God who raised up Moses. It was God who raised up Pharaoh. It was God who orchestrated the plagues. It was God who brought the Israelites through the Red Sea. It was God who destroyed Pharaoh's army in the sea. God was worthy of praise, for it was he who delivered his people. This would be the theme for Israel's praise. The exodus would be the memory for Jewish worship.

This event addresses the substance of worship: Our worship is not to celebrate what we do but what God does. This is how the Jewish mind understood the purpose of worship although straying from this purpose repeatedly.

The unfaithfulness of Israel could be an exegetical lens with which to read the Old Testament. However, the real theme is God's love. "I will betroth you to Me forever; Yes, I will betroth you to Me/In righteousness and justice, in lovingkindness and mercy; I will betroth you to Me in faithfulness, and you shall know the LORD" (Hosea 2:19–20 NKJV). God is romancing his people; he is trying to get our attention so that we might turn and worship him, thereby finding ultimate fulfillment.

The psalmist used this event to compose his songs and constantly referred back to how God delivered Israel from Egypt. This is a reminder of God's faithfulness during times of distress. Psalm 106:7–12 says:

When our fathers were in Egypt,
  they gave no thought to
  your miracles;
they did not remember your
  many kindnesses,
  and they rebelled by the sea,
  the Red Sea.
Yet he saved them for his name's
  sake,
  to make his mighty power
  known.
He rebuked the Red Sea, and it
  dried up;
  he led them through the depths
  as through a desert.
He saved them from the hand
  of the foe;
  from the hand of the enemy he
  redeemed them.
The waters covered their
  adversaries;
  not one of them survived,
Then they believed his promises
  and sang his praise.

The Psalms are filled with an appreciation for the God who redeems his people. In Psalm 136, we are commanded to give thanks to the Lord for his goodness. Starting in verse 10, the psalmist begins the history of the exodus. "To him who struck down the firstborn of Egypt (his love endures forever) / and brought Israel out from among them . . . / with a mighty hand and outstretched arm . . . / to him who divided the Red Sea asunder . . . / and brought Israel through the midst of it . . . / but swept Pharaoh and his army into the Red Sea" (Ps. 136:10–15).

Redemption is the key theme for the worship leader. David Peterson states: "Decisive for understanding the Old

Testament view of worship is the idea that the God of heaven and earth had taken the initiative in making himself known, first to the patriarchs of Israel and then, through the events of the exodus from Egypt and encounter on Mount Sinai, to the nation as a whole."[2]

To develop into the complete worship leader, it is imperative that we remember God's redemptive acts. To become theologians, we must major in the message of redemption. We must return to the themes of atonement, propitiation, and justification, which are magnified in the New Testament.

THE SCRIPTURES AND CHRISTOCENTRIC WORSHIP

God's special revelation is culminated in the Christ events. What the exodus was for Jewish worship, the Christ events are for Christian worship. "You shall call His name Jesus, for He will save His people from their sins" (Matt. 1:21 NKJV). God's desire to bring complete redemption is found in the saving work of his Messiah, Jesus Christ. The works of Robert Webber have emphasized this aspect of worship:

> I was discussing with Henry Jauhiainen the idea that worship celebrates the Christ-event. He summarized the point very well: "Worship often degenerated into celebrating the believer's dedication to God. After a while you wake up and say, 'Hey, what are we celebrating here? Not my dedication. We're celebrating the work of Christ!'"
>
> Pastor Jauhiainen's point is extremely important. We don't go to worship to celebrate what we have done. We don't say, "Look, Lord, isn't it wonderful that I believe in you, follow you, and serve you!" No! We go to worship to praise and thank God for what he has done, is doing, and will do.[3]

It is common in modern evangelicalism to produce worship that is human centered. We often come to celebrate and honor what we have done; the church calendar is eclipsed by the secular calendar. From Advent, Christmas, Epiphany, Lent, Easter, Ascension, and Pentecost, we move to Mother's Day, Father's Day, Memorial Day, and the Fourth of July. We celebrate who we are and what we do instead of who God is and what he does. If there was ever a need for reformation, it is in our worship services in America. We have replaced the rightful worship of God with the worship of ourselves.

Throughout history this has been a problem. The Bible is clear that from the beginning of human life, a person is depraved and not a worshiper of the living God (see Gen. 6:5; 1 Kings 8:46; Pss. 51:3–5; 53:3; Prov. 20:9; Isa. 53:6; 64:6, 7; Rom. 1:18–32; 1 John 1:8). It is true, as mentioned in the previous chapter, that every human being is a worshiper of something. Yet every human being has chosen to replace the rightful object of worship for something else. Such worship is unacceptable because it is not directed to God, who alone is holy. How do we approach a holy God? God has provided the answer to this question in his Word: We need a representative who offers worship on our behalf. In the Old Testament, this representative was the high priest, the only one who had access to the Holy of Holies. The high priest made intercession and atonement for the people he represented. There were numerous requirements for this position. But these priests were only a foreshadowing of Jesus Christ, the High Priest who would live forever to make intercession. This is an excellent place to discuss the distinctiveness of Christian worship.

What makes Christian worship distinctive from Jewish worship is the role of Jesus Christ as High Priest. James B. Torrance in an article entitled "The Place of Jesus Christ in Worship" states,

> The good news of the Gospel is that Jesus comes to be the Priest of Creation, to do for men what man fails to do, to

offer to God the worship and the praise that we have failed to offer, to glorify God by a life of perfect obedience, to be the One true servant of the Lord, in whom and through whom we are renewed in the image of God and in the worship of God.[4]

Jesus is our High Priest and therefore represents us before the Father. It is through Jesus Christ that our worship is acceptable to the Father. Torrance again unveils this truth when he states:

> Such is the wonderful love of God, that he has come to us in Jesus Christ, and in Jesus assumed our life (the life of all men), underwritten our responsibilities, offered for us a life of worship and obedience and prayer to the Father, taken to Himself our body of death, vicariously submitted for us to the verdict of "guilty," died our death and rose again in our humanity, so that by the grace of God, His life is our life, His death is our death, His victory our victory, His resurrection our resurrection, His righteousness our righteousness and His eternal prayer and self-offerings to the Father our prayer and offering in the presence of the Father. So we are accepted in the Beloved, and discover our status as sons.[5]

We speak of the imputed righteousness concerning our justification; namely through faith in Jesus Christ, his righteousness becomes ours. Yet we often fail to make the connection as it pertains to worship. Through faith in Jesus, our worship is made acceptable to the Father. The Book of Hebrews brings out this theology; listen to what the writer says beginning in chapter four, verse fourteen:

> Therefore, since we have a great high priest who has gone through the heavens, Jesus the Son of God, let us hold firmly to the faith we profess. For we do not have a high priest who is unable to sympathize with our weaknesses,

but we have one who has been tempted in every way, just as we are—yet was without sin. Let us then approach the throne of grace with confidence, so that we may receive mercy and find grace to help us in our time of need. Every high priest is selected from among men and is appointed to represent them in matters related to God, to offer gifts and sacrifices for sins. He is able to deal gently with those who are ignorant and are going astray, since he himself is subject to weakness.

HEBREWS 4:14–5:2

We are encouraged to approach the throne of grace with confidence. We are free to worship the living God. Because of who we are in Jesus, we can come before the Father. This is a tremendous truth for Christians. As believers in Jesus Christ we need to get this deep into our souls. This one truth alone is why I am a worshiper of the living God. Outside of Christ I am nothing. My worship of God is poor, deficient, and unacceptable to a Holy God. Because I have a High Priest ever living to make intercession for me, I can come before God and call out, "Abba, Father." This is good news and should spark a desire for worship. The writer of Hebrews concludes this wonderful theology of worship by exhorting us with a word on how to respond to God: "Through Jesus, therefore, let us continually offer to God a sacrifice of praise—the fruit of lips that confess his name" (Heb. 13:15). I frequently tell our musicians that if they accidentally make a mistake, they shouldn't be discouraged, because Christ's worship on our behalf is perfect.

As I think of Christ-centered worship, I am reminded of the song "Jesus, Name Above All Names": "Jesus name above all names, beautiful Savior, glorious Lord. Emmanuel, God is with us. Blessed Redeemer, Living Word."[6] It is because of what Jesus has done that we as Christians can even discuss the topic of worship. If Jesus had not ascended, no outpouring of the Holy Spirit would have happened.

And it is this outpouring that enables us as believers to worship together; the Holy Spirit brings us together in unity.

When we examine the content of the hymns in the New Testament, it is clear that Christ was the center of these hymns. The apostle Paul in particular had a clear understanding of why Christ had come to this world. He came to save his people from their sins. Ralph Martin states:

> The "hymns" preserved in the Pauline churches took a Christological turn and were exclusively devoted to a recital of the "events of salvation" wrought out in the mission and achievement of Jesus. The New Testament teaching on the person of Christ is virtually contained in those passages most likely to be classified as early hymns of the church: John 1:1–18; Philippians 2:6–11; Colossians 1:15–20; 1 Timothy 3:16. The common feature that unites these sublime texts, even if they derive from a variety of church situations, is their interest in the preincarnate Lord who came to reveal the Father and to restore a lost creation. The link-term connecting revelation and cosmic renewal is redemption. At the cost of his life given over to the will of God in sacrifice and self-offering, Jesus died the sinner's death and released those forces into human experience that make possible a true basis for forgiveness of sins and new life. But the message, though authenticated in human experience as a reconciliation to God, has wider ramifications. It proclaims a new world set right with its creator, the overthrow of evil powers, and a fresh start to human history that will eventually lead to a universe restored to its pristine glory and harmony. The sweep of these hymns is as vast as that world in whose ultimate destiny no refractory or alien elements are permitted to continue. The New Testament hymns tremble on the verge of a cosmic Jubilee when God will be "all in all" (1 Cor. 15:28) as all things are brought under the sole headship of the reigning Christ (Eph. 1:10).[7]

If the New Testament hymns celebrated the Christ events, how much more should our hymns and praise songs celebrate Christ? Part of becoming a complete worship leader is keeping in mind that redemption is the heart of our songs. As we are composing or selecting choir anthems for the upcoming year, let us look for music that celebrates Christ. Let us look for material that will bring people to the cross. It is Christ who must be celebrated. It is before him that we bring our offerings.[8]

THE GOD OF THE SCRIPTURES INITIATES WORSHIP

One of the distinctives of evangelical worship is the role that the Scriptures play in our worship services. Worship is our response to what God has revealed about himself. The Scriptures are the written record where we receive God's special revelation. Through the Scriptures, we learn about God; we learn about his love for his people; and we discover his redemptive plan. Worship is our response to this foundational truth. It is important that the Scriptures take a top priority in our worship services. The reading and preaching from the Bible must be emphasized, and when we offer prayer, the Scriptures should form the content of our appeal to God.

We should also include songs that contain the Scriptures. We have to get beyond the criteria that only ask whether or not this is an inspiring tune, whether it has a great beat, or whether the arrangement will work. I am not diminishing the importance of musical excellence; we will talk about this in part three. But as we evaluate worship musically, we need to be asking if it is scriptural.[9] I recently asked Buddy Owens from Maranatha Music what criteria he uses for selecting a song for Promise Keepers. His response was threefold: Is it scriptural? Is it easy to learn? Is it hard to forget? Notice the first: Is it scriptural?

Worship devoid of scriptural influence will degenerate into idolatry. We must return to the Scriptures if our worship is to undergo reform. We need a reformation that would cry out "Sola Scriptura." J. I. Packer states:

> Christianity is the true worship and service of the true God, mankind's Creator and Redeemer. It is a religion that rests on revelation: nobody would know the truth about God, nor be able to relate to Him in a personal way, had God not first acted to make Himself known. But God has so acted, and the sixty-six books of the Bible, thirty-nine written before Christ came and twenty-seven after, are together the record, interpretation, and expression of His self-disclosure. God and godliness are the Bible's uniting themes.
>
> The idea of written directives from God Himself as a basis for godly living goes back to God's inscribing the Ten Commandments on stone tablets and prompting Moses to write His laws and the history of His dealings with His people (Exod. 32:15, 16; 34:1, 27, 28; Num. 33:2; Deut. 31:9).
>
> Digesting and living by this material was always central to true devotion for both leaders and others in Israel (Josh. 1:7, 8; 2 Kings 17:13; 22:8–13; 1 Chron. 22:12,13; Neh. 8; Ps. 119), and the principle that all must be governed by the Scriptures has passed into Christianity.
>
> What Scripture says, God says; for, in a manner comparable only to the deeper mystery of the Incarnation, the Bible is both fully human and fully divine. So all its manifold contents—histories, prophecies, poems, songs, wisdom writings, sermons, statistics, letter, and whatever else—should be received as from God, and all that biblical writers teach should be revered as God's authoritative instruction. Christians should be grateful to God for the gift of His written Word, and conscientious in basing their faith and life entirely and exclusively upon it.[10]

The complete worship leader must conform to the written Word of God. The Bible must be our compass as we lead others in worship. We cannot afford to eradicate the

Scriptures from our proclamation; indeed, they should govern every moment of the worship service from the prelude to the postlude. People should come into our church and encounter the people of God and the revelation of God. It is through the proclamation of the Word that the unchurched will meet the living Christ: "How beautiful are the feet of those who preach the gospel of peace, Who bring glad tidings of good things! . . . So then faith comes by hearing, and hearing by the word of God" (Rom. 10:15, 17 NKJV).

If faith is absent in our church, it is because ignorance of the Scriptures is escalating. Missionaries are laboring to translate the Word of God in new languages. Yet in our country where translations abound, the word is habitually neglected. This is a great tragedy in the modern church. As a result, we are producing people who lack faith because they don't know the Word of God.

If you want to be a complete worship leader, fall in love with the Scriptures and the author of the Scriptures. Pray and sing over the Scriptures. Get the Word of God deep in your soul. Then articulate with clarity the hope that is within you. This is what it means to worship the Lord with accuracy.

There are other places to permeate the Word into the body of Christ. The small group, Sunday school, or one-on-one discipleship time can be an effective place to teach the Bible. The more we encourage the body of Christ to be in the Word throughout the week, the more we will see that Word develop worshipers. The more we encourage the church to study the Word, the more they will respond with praise and thanksgiving.

Small groups, in particular, should study the Word. The trend in small groups today is therapy, but if this consumes our church groups, we will not produce people who respond to the Word. How can one respond to the Word (worship) without studying it? The small group must be used strategically to develop worshipers of the living God.

Study and response should be engaged in the Sunday school class and the one-on-one discipleship time as well. Worship need not be left to the 9:00 or the 10:30 hour. The Word and worship produce the perfect duet in all of our ministries.

REDEMPTION CELEBRATED THROUGH THE LORD'S SUPPER AND BAPTISM

We also celebrate the special revelation that God has brought through participation in the Lord's Supper and baptism. When we come to the Lord's table we are commemorating what Christ did for us on the cross. As we partake of the elements, we are remembering and responding to what Christ has done for us; we are celebrating the Christ events.[11]

In baptism, we are celebrating new life in Christ Jesus. We are declaring that by his death we too have died. And through his resurrection, we have newness of life. We are worshiping the risen Lord as a new creation. What a beautiful demonstration of the life we have in Jesus.

REPRISE

God has revealed himself through what he has created and through his redemptive acts. Throughout history, God has been pursuing his people. He is tenaciously reaching out to the human race. Historically, redemption has been the primer for worship. Our understanding of God's redemptive acts is crucial if we are going to become complete worship leaders.

The nation of Israel celebrated the fact that God had redeemed his people from Egypt. The exodus was the climax

44

of worship for the Jews. Memorizing the Psalms is boot camp for prayer and worship, because in this collection we see the exodus event told again and again. Redemption from the bondage of Egypt was the greatest reason to give God praise and thanksgiving.

For the Christian, the Christ events have become the climax of worship and should have a dominant role in our worship services. Redemption comes through Jesus Christ; salvation from the wrath of God is the theme of the Christian's song. We celebrate Christ's resurrection, for in his resurrection is our resurrection.

Furthermore, we celebrate what God is doing today and what he will do in the future. This is the song of revival we long for and need; it is also the theme of our preaching. We acknowledge that redemption is not over; we can see God moving in the world. Just imagine if God decided to stop calling people from every tribe and nation: Billions of people would spend eternity in hell. Yet we know that God is gracious and that he is moving among the nations, working in the hearts of men and women to bring them into a relationship with Jesus Christ. We need to remember that God is not finished. Therefore, we as worship leaders should include prayer for revival in our services.

May we learn how to celebrate what God has done, is doing, and will do when he consummates his redemptive plan. Our worship is not about us but about God. We proclaim Christ, not ourselves. It is all about what God has done, is doing, and will do. "For we do not preach ourselves, but Jesus Christ as Lord" (2 Cor. 4:5).

So we conclude with part one. If we are to be effective as worship leaders, we must renew our love for theology. Theology gives us the motive, the language, and the reason for worshiping the living God. We don't initiate worship; God does. He has revealed himself through creation and redemption, and these two themes must weave in and out of our liturgy.

In part two we will look at what it means to become a disciple. It is important to know that God has revealed himself and that he has redeemed us. Yet we must experience this firsthand. For the worship leader to be complete, he or she must understand and experience the gospel. Only then will the worship leader worship in spirit and truth.

BECOMING
A DISCIPLE

INTRODUCTION
TO PART TWO

IN PART ONE, I discussed the importance of becoming a theologian as foundational to becoming a complete worship leader. The worship leader must think theologically about what he or she is doing and must worship God with accuracy. Worship is initiated by God who has revealed himself. Theology is discovering God, not inventing religion. Revelation tells us three bits of information: There is a God, we have rebelled against this God, and we need to be redeemed.

In part two, I will discuss the continuation of this story as it pertains to worship leadership. We must be born again and become disciples of Jesus Christ if we are to see worship produced by the Spirit. True worship will ultimately come from hearts that have been regenerated by the Spirit of Christ. The complete worship leader must not only become a theologian but a disciple. We must worship God with accuracy and with integrity. We must understand redemptive history and become *participants* in the gospel story.

In chapter three, I will discuss the topic of salvation (in its total process), which is the fundamental prerequisite for *true* worship. Worship is not just the songs we sing but our position in Christ and the narrative of the Christian life. In chapter four, I will discuss the topic of proclamation. Whether through behavior, word, or art, proclamation is what we do when Christ is at work in our lives. In these chapters, we will move beyond the knowledge that is so important for us as worship leaders, to the issues of experience, behavior, and obedience as they pertain to becoming vessels of worship. Ultimately, worship comes from worshipers. Christian worship comes from those who know, love, and follow Christ.

three

SALVATION

As we saw in chapter two, unregenerate people are inca-
pable of worshiping the living God for they are too busy
worshiping themselves or something else. We worship what
we desire. If the lost do not desire God they are not going
to worship him.[1]

> The fool has said in his heart,
> "There is no God."
> They are corrupt,
> They have done abominable works,
> There is none who does good.
>
> The LORD looks down from heaven
>   upon the children of men,
> To see if there are any who
>   understand, who seek God.
>
> They have all turned aside,
> They have together become corrupt;
> There is none who does good,
> No, not one.
>
> PSALM 14:1–3 NKJV

We need an interruption to this depravity if we are going to become worshipers of the living God. Jesus said: "Unless one is born again, he cannot see the kingdom of God" (John 3:3 NKJV). It is the Spirit who brings new life. It is not our programs, our techniques, our buildings, our personalities, or our style of worship. It is the Spirit of God that causes people to be born again.

Jesus stated that "The wind blows where it wishes, and you hear the sound of it, but cannot tell where it comes from and where it goes. So is everyone who is born of the Spirit" (John 3:8 NKJV). This regeneration process is Spirit-initiated and Spirit-consummated. Titus 3:5 tells us that "He saved us, not on the basis of deeds which we have done in righteousness, but according to His mercy, by the washing of regeneration and renewing by the Holy Spirit" (NASB). It is the Holy Spirit who produces worshipers of the living God.

As worship leaders we must get two things straight. If we are to lead in worship, we ourselves must be born again. And, if our congregations are to worship, they must be born again. This is so basic, yet greatly neglected in churches across America. If we are wondering why worship is cold in some of our churches, it is a possibility that our people are not born again.

What are the indicators of regeneration? First, have you confessed with your mouth that Jesus is Lord? Do you believe in your heart that God raised him from the dead? "With the heart man believes, resulting in righteousness, and with the mouth he confesses, resulting in salvation" (Rom. 10:10 NASB).

Second, do you see evidence that the Spirit lives within you? Is there fruit? "The fruit of the Spirit is love, joy, peace, longsuffering, kindness, goodness, faithfulness, gentleness, self-control" (Gal. 5:22–23 NKJV). Have you *experienced* the Spirit of God in your life? Gordon Fee in his book *Paul, the Spirit, and the People of God* states that "salvation in Christ is not simply a theological truth, predicated on God's prior action and the historical work of Christ. Salvation is an experienced reality, made so by the person of the Spirit coming into our lives. One simply cannot be a Christian in any Pauline sense without the effective work of the Trinity.[2]

We cannot lead congregational worship if we do not have a relationship with the One whom we worship. We will promote hypocrisy. God desires those who will worship him in spirit and in truth. We can do neither if we are not born again. We must settle this issue immediately.

We should not expect an unbeliever to worship God. If people in our congregation are not born again, how can we expect them to worship? I am not saying that they will not attend a worship service. I am saying that they have no intrinsic capability for true worship.

One thing that will ignite your worship services is to see people saved on a regular basis. When God is at work, enthusiasm is high. We need to see people coming to Christ. We need to see people understanding as well as *experiencing* the gospel. We need to have revival if we are going to have dynamic worship services. Dead hearts cannot produce dynamic worship, but hearts that are passionate about Jesus will make any worship service exciting. Therefore, we desperately need the work of the Holy Spirit, who will breathe new life into lifeless liturgy.

SOTERIOS AND THE WORSHIP LEADER

The New Testament uses the term salvation (*soterios*) in many different tenses. There is a sense in which we were saved (from the foundation of the world); we were being saved (by the work of God in history); we are saved (by being in the justified state); we are being saved (by being sanctified or made holy); and we will be saved (by experiencing the consummation of our redemption in heaven).

Understanding how this word *salvation* is used is crucial for the worship leader.

The trend in evangelical worship is to emphasize justification and glorification. If you look at an evangelical hymnal, you will notice the hymns are dominated by these two themes. In contrast, pentecostal/charismatic worship tends to emphasize sanctification. Most of the praise choruses are driven by the themes of renewal and revival and focus on what the Holy Spirit is doing today. This is a good emphasis. Yet when sanctification is emphasized to the point that you never sing or speak about what Christ has already done, this is not good. The same imbalance can be found in evangelical worship with its underemphasis on sanctification.

The balance will come when worship leaders are reminded that the thread of redemption has begun, is going on, and will be consummated when Christ returns. We need to sing about what Christ has done, to implore the Holy Spirit through prayer and song to move in our midst today, and to remind ourselves that we are resident aliens passing through this world. This will give a balanced perspective to our worship services.

JUSTIFICATION

I have mentioned as worship leaders we must be born again and that the people whom we seek to lead in worship must be born again. When we use the term *justification*, we are speaking of our legal position in Christ. Are we guilty or acquitted? Romans 5:1–2a, 9–11 states:

> Therefore, since we have been justified through faith, we have peace with God through our Lord Jesus Christ, through whom we have gained access by faith into this grace in which we now stand. . . . Since we have now been justified by his blood, how much more shall we be saved

from God's wrath through him! For if, when we were God's enemies, we were reconciled to him through the death of his Son, how much more, having been reconciled, shall we be saved through his life! Not only is this so, but we also rejoice in God through our Lord Jesus Christ, through whom we have now received reconciliation.

Before we were in a justified state, we were God's enemies, not his worshipers. From God's perspective, we were rebellious. He considers the unregenerate his enemies. The only thing awaiting the rebel is God's wrath (v. 9).

Unfortunately, this message has been eclipsed by a postmodern culture that campaigns for tolerance at any cost. Although the government of the United States gives us the right to be theologically wrong, God never gives us that right. Only born again, regenerate saints are candidates for true worship that is acceptable to God.

In being reconciled to God "we have peace with God" (Rom. 5:1). The key to understanding this verse is the preposition. Paul did not say that we have the peace *of* God. No; he said that we have peace *with* God. Again, when we were justified, we turned from being God's enemies to being at peace *with* him. This is of paramount importance concerning the topic of worship.

The justified position is available only in Christ, through faith. "Salvation is found in no one else, for there is no other name under heaven given to men by which we must be saved" (Acts 4:12). It is through his perfect, obedient life, his death, his resurrection, and his ascension that salvation is made possible.

The worship lifestyle is impossible without being born again. If there is no regeneration, there will be no worship of the living God. There will be worship, but this worship will not be to the God of the Bible. Our understanding of justification is fundamental and foundational for Christian worship.

THE MERCY OF GOD, REGENERATION, AND RENEWAL

In the previous section I discussed the justified state and why acquiring this position is fundamental to worship. In this section, I would like to elaborate not so much on *what* needs to take place but on *how* it takes place. Once again, Titus 3:5 tells us, "He saved us, not on the basis of deeds which we have done in righteousness, but according to His mercy, by the washing of regeneration and renewing by the Holy Spirit" (NASB).

We learn from this passage that salvation is according to God's mercy. He is not obligated to anyone. He shows himself to be merciful toward some and just toward others. He is never unjust. In Romans 9 the apostle Paul goes into great detail about how God is the author of our salvation. If God was obligated to be merciful to everyone, would it then be mercy?

Universalism is prevalent in our Christian thought today. Yet Jesus himself discussed the topic of hell more than anyone else in the Bible. If we are not recipients of the mercy of God, we will be recipients of the wrath of God! Those of us who are born again have every incentive to thank, praise, and worship God. We are recipients of God's mercy, not because of deeds done in righteousness but simply because of his mercy.[3]

Next in this Scripture passage is the issue of the washing of regeneration and renewal of the Holy Spirit. In other words, the washing of regeneration is only possible when we have been renewed by the Holy Spirit. We are washed from our sins and brought to life. We are cleansed from our transgressions and given an inheritance in the kingdom of God.

This means everything when we speak of worship, because the new life brought about by the Spirit of God is what gives us the ability to become worshipers of the living God. Only when we are quickened by this wonderful life can we learn what praise and worship are all about.

SALVATION AS SANCTIFICATION

Once we have been born again, we should begin to see the fruit of the new life. This process of becoming like Christ is called sanctification. If we are truly God's people we will grow in becoming like Christ. If we do not see any fruit in our life, we should be concerned if we are born again.

Jesus says that if you are going to be his disciple you must take up your cross daily and follow him (see Luke 9:23). You cannot be a worshiper of the living God and continue as though you were unregenerate. God will have nothing to do with it (see Rom. 6:1–14).

If you can answer yes to the following questions, it is probable that you are a true worshiper of God. Honestly evaluate yourself in light of these questions.

First of all, do you love the Lord passionately? Jesus reaffirmed this imperative of Deuteronomy 6 when he said in Matthew 22:37–40 that this commandment was the summation of all of the law and the prophets. If you can answer in the affirmative, praise the Lord. If not, you need to find out where your treasure is, for "where your treasure is, there your heart will be also" (Matt. 6:21). Worship leader, it might be that you love music more than God. Music, like other art forms, is to be used to love God. God is not to be used to love music. That is idolatry. The issue that you need to settle in your heart is what or whom do you love?

Second, do you have a love for the Word of God? All of God's covenant people must pledge allegiance not only to God but also to what he has declared to be true as taught in the Holy Scriptures. Jesus said in John 14:21, "He who has My commandments and keeps them, he it is who loves

Me, and he who loves Me shall be loved by My Father, and I will love him and will disclose Myself to him" (NASB). The prerequisite for obeying the Word is to know what it teaches. We cannot be biblically illiterate.

Third, do you exemplify the fruit of the Spirit in your life? The fruit of the Spirit is not a list of moral qualities that you study and memorize; rather, it is what should be empirically evident as the result of the Spirit of God living within. If you have the Spirit of God, you will reflect these qualities to some degree. If however, you do not have the Spirit of God, "the acts of the sinful nature are obvious: sexual immorality, impurity and debauchery; idolatry and witchcraft; hatred, discord, jealousy, fits of rage, selfish ambition, dissensions, factions and envy; drunkenness, orgies, and the like. I warn you, as I did before, that those who live like this will not inherit the kingdom of God" (Gal. 5:19–21). Paul states that we will exemplify either the acts of the sinful nature or the fruit of the Spirit.

If you have a love for God, a love for the Word, and are exemplifying the fruit of the Spirit in your life, it is probable that you are engaged in the other disciplines as well such as prayer and fellowship. If you are becoming like Christ, you are also engaged in Christian worship. On the other hand, if you are not becoming like Christ, you are not worshiping God. The questions in the simple checklist that I have given can be thought of as indicators that the Spirit of God lives within you.[4]

SALVATION AND THE LIFESTYLE OF WORSHIP

I have argued that for one to be a worshiper of the living God, one must be born again and controlled by the Spirit of God. It is ultimately God's people who become worshipers of him. Only those who have experienced salvation from the living God learn what it means to worship him.

During my devotional life, I reflect on what God has done for me. This motivates me to praise God with everything that is within me. It is not just the story of redemption that excites me; it is the reality that the story of redemption has invaded my personal life. It is the reality that I am one of the characters in God's glorious plan: the salvation of a depraved human being who is daily being transformed into a worshiper of the living God. I am a worshiper because of the love of God. I am a worship leader because I have personally experienced the essence of true worship: salvation.

If our personal experience of salvation motivates us as worship leaders to praise God, this will be contagious to the congregation. The body of Christ can sense when a worship leader is excited about Christ. They can tell the worship leader who really appreciates the love of Christ from the worship leader who is in love with their voice or some other human quality. As you will see in a moment, I am not undermining the importance of musical excellence. However, if that is all that is in your heart, your worship is idolatrous. All that will be revealed will be music, not Jesus. We need to be passionately in love with the Savior. We need to be infatuated with Jesus Christ.

As a worship leader, remind yourself, your praise team, your choir, your orchestra, and whomever else you work with, that the reason we get up every Sunday morning is to declare to the world that Jesus lives and that salvation is available to those who have faith in him.

The Personal Testimony and Worship

Try scheduling personal testimonies in your worship services. Start with yourself, with the elders and deacons, or with your musicians. Have one person get up each week and share what Jesus is doing in his or her life. Then do this with other members of your congregation. Three things will happen. First, people will be reminded why we sing to the Lord Sunday after Sunday. Second, they will be blessed by the testimony of their brother or sister and how God is working in his or her life. Third, others will be inspired to adopt a Great Commission lifestyle.

As an example, we recently had a couple share in our worship service how God had restored their marriage. Both had gone to a Christian college and were engaged and married soon after graduating. Not long after their wedding, trouble began to brew in their marriage. Eventually there was an affair. In the midst of this situation, they decided to get some help. The couple who counseled them ended up leading them both into a personal relationship with Jesus Christ. Neither of them had been born again. Discipleship and marriage counseling then followed, and God healed their marriage.

When this couple shared their story in our service, God's presence was felt in a special way. We all came away realizing that one can be religious and not know God. We were reminded of the healing power of Christ and his desire to restore broken people.

Not everyone has to have a 700 Club testimony. Some people will share a testimony of how they have suffered and how in the darkest time, only God was able to sustain them. This too can be a blessing to the body of Christ. Testimonies ignite worship services.

REPRISE

Worship is not a subject to be studied void of a personal relationship with the living God. Worship is something that is lived out by the people who have been redeemed by the blood of the Lamb. It is something that adopted sons and daughters engage in to celebrate the fact that they have been saved from the wrath of God. May we always remember that we sing because we have a song to sing, namely the praise of being redeemed by Jesus Christ.

---
four

PROCLAMATION

IN ADDITION TO EXPERIENCING SALVATION, worship
leaders tell others what God has done throughout history
and what Christ is currently doing and will do in the future.
Proclamation is taking place at all times. This is the role
of a worship leader.

There is nothing more powerful than a worship leader
who is being mastered by the message. When he or she
knows the gospel, is passionate about the gospel, and is
articulate about the gospel, that worship leader will have
a great impact on many lives. The opposite is also true. When
the worship leader is promoting another agenda besides
the gospel, the worship will be diluted.

Discipleship is the experience of salvation and the telling
of good news. The disciple should always be generous with
the good news. All of Christ's disciples are to be ambassadors. The apostle Paul states that "we are therefore Christ's
ambassadors" (2 Cor. 5:20). We represent Jesus Christ and
the kingdom of God.

In a Christian worship service born-again people declare
through song, sacraments, and Word what Christ has done.
We gather Sunday after Sunday to proclaim Jesus Christ

and what he has accomplished throughout history. This is Christian worship. We must preach Christ and Christ alone. We must proclaim his life, death, resurrection, ascension, and second coming if our worship services are to be Christ centered.[1]

How do we proclaim Christ? How do we declare the living Word? How do we communicate that Jesus is the King of kings and Lord of lords? What are the elements that are characteristic to proclamation?

Proclaiming Christ through Our Behavior

The first way we proclaim Christ is by the way we live; our behavior should distinguish us as Christians. Oftentimes we focus so much on having correct doctrine and pay little attention about how to live. We make the acid test of Christianity belief in information and ignore the great imperative given by our Lord Jesus Christ, "A new command I give you: Love one another. As I have loved you, so you must love one another. By this all men will know that you are my disciples, if you love one another" (John 13:34–35). Our love for people will proclaim Christ more than anything else we do.

I am not stating that doctrine and theology are unimportant (I spent the first two chapters arguing that they are important). Christianity *is* rational. It is important that we are able to say with the apostle Paul, "if any man is preaching to you a gospel contrary to that which you received, let him be accursed" (Gal. 1:9 NASB), concerning the basic tenets of Christianity. Yet, one of the marks of this Christianity according to Jesus himself is that love permeates our behavior.

A worship leader must demonstrate love. If we have wonderful musical skills, rhetoric, and liturgy but do not have love, we amount to nothing (see 1 Cor. 13). It is not enough to be eloquent. We must exemplify love in our behavior. "Love is patient, love is kind. It does not envy, it does not boast, it is not proud. It is not rude, it is not self-seeking, it is not easily angered, it keeps no record of wrongs. Love does not delight in evil but rejoices with the truth. It always protects, always trusts, always hopes, always perseveres" (1 Cor. 13:4–7). This is the kind of Christianity we should proclaim as worship leaders. Love should permeate all that we do.

There is a phrase that states, "who you are speaks so loudly that I cannot hear what you are saying." Are you proclaiming Christ in your behavior or are you proclaiming something else? It is important for you to determine what is driving you as a worship leader.

It is absolutely imperative that we proclaim Christ by living the way he did. We should reflect the fruit of the Spirit consistently in our lives. This is the kind of message that should come through our worship leadership. We should be skilled artists but godly people, believers that reflect the indwelling Spirit.

The primary means that the gospel is revealed is in how we behave before a watching world. We are the message, not just the songs we sing or the messages we preach.

Physical and Emotional Health as Proclamation

If we lead out of who we are, then we as worship leaders must take care of our health. It is imperative that we get enough rest and exercise to be our best in attitude and behavior. It is also important to watch the kinds of food we put into our bodies. We all know that a poor diet will contribute to poor health and that *intentional* poor health is not a good witness for the gospel.

When I do not get the rest and exercise I need, I am inevitably irritated and quick to react negatively to stressful situations. I already have an enemy working overtime so that I might misrepresent Jesus in my behavior. The last thing I need is to help the devil out. I need to take good care of my physical body so that I might proclaim Jesus in my being.

A related concern to physical health is how we are guarding our emotional health. Emotional health is certainly dependent on having good physical health. But there are other issues, such as not forgiving people, not taking a day of rest, taking on too many responsibilities, becoming unfocused, not having a life-mission statement, having poor financial management skills, and not having good interpersonal relationships. These can be a strain on our emotional health. We need to stay on top of issues that would supply unnecessary stress to our lives. It is these basic issues that contribute to a poor testimony for the gospel. We as worship leaders need self-control and peace in our lives; we must represent the life and easy yoke that Jesus spoke about in Matthew 11:28–30.

PROCLAIMING CHRIST THROUGH YOUR MARRIAGE AND FAMILY

If you are married, whether you realize it or not, your marriage is a testimony for the gospel. As a worship leader, you must invest in your relationship with your spouse. This is imperative for your testimony. The last thing that you need hindering your ministry is a deteriorating marriage.

The same is true if you have children. Invest in your kids. Worship with your children. Teach them the Word of God. Pray *with* them. Pray *for* them. Whatever you do in the ministry, make sure that you do not neglect your family. Do not be another statistic of someone who had to step down from the ministry because of family problems. Give your life to the Lord first; then give your heart to your family. A healthy marriage and God-honoring children will give you momentum as a worship leader quicker than anything else.[2]

PROCLAIMING CHRIST IN LANGUAGE

We also proclaim Christ when we speak. The language we use as worship leaders is of utmost importance. We simply cannot afford to be flippant, indiscreet, or thoughtless in the words we use. Our words must clearly, succinctly say something about the gospel.

It has been said that music is a powerful indoctrination tool. This is true in secular music, but it is especially true in Christian music. The words we sing will sink deep into the souls of people, and it is imperative that we have thought through what we want to communicate.

Grace in Our Conversations

"Let your conversation be always full of grace, seasoned with salt, so that you may know how to answer everyone" (Col. 4:6). We have a tendency in our conversations to either exalt ourselves or put other people down; we slander, gossip, criticize, and destroy other people in our speech. James tells us that "the tongue is a small part of the body, but it makes great boasts. Consider what a great forest is set on fire by a small spark. The tongue also is a fire, a world of evil among the parts of the body. It corrupts the whole person, sets the whole course of his life on fire, and is itself set on fire by hell" (James 3:5–6).

We worship leaders need to allow the Holy Spirit to control our speech so that it might be characterized by grace. What is meant by the phrase "Let your conversation be always full of grace"? First, it means that we speak of the goodness of God. If we cultivate habits of thanksgiving, we will not whine and bicker. If we are constantly making our boast in the Lord, we will have little time for displaying a grumbling spirit.

Second, it has to do with the way we speak to others and about others. We need to be gracious, kind, and full of goodness when we speak to one another. If you put one human being with another human being, there will be friction. Courtesy is the lubricant in interpersonal relationships. Every time we interact with another human being with civility, the relationship will be enhanced.

In our speech we must also honor those who are not present. It is hypocritical to declare that we love God and then verbally murder a brother or sister with slanderous speech.

For you to be a complete worship leader, you must be known for your speech being full of grace, seasoned with salt. Your speech should bring healing, restoration, and hope; it should not be full of murmuring, whining, or complaining. As a worship leader, you must be characterized by your ability to proclaim the gospel at all times. This will then be congruent with the songs you sing.

The Words We Sing

We need to think about the words we say but also about the words we sing. Do the words in our songs, both choruses and hymns, say something about Jesus? Are we proclaiming the gospel in our songs? This is important. For me it is a more pressing issue than whether we use guitars, drums, choirs, or organs. The means to communicate the message is important, but the message itself is more important.

Many songs, both traditional and contemporary, are not worthy of being in a church service. They either do not say anything or they convey the wrong message about the gospel. We need to know the message well enough that when a new song comes across our desk, we have the discernment to accept or reject it based on the text alone. The same is true in our own compositions. We need to write

words that have gospel integrity and avoid writing mis-
leading words about our God. We need to reflect the Lord
in the texts that we compose.

The words do not necessarily have to be elaborate in order
to communicate the simplicity of the gospel. Paul stated:

> When I came to you, brothers, I did not come with elo-
> quence or superior wisdom as I proclaimed to you the tes-
> timony about God. For I resolved to know nothing while
> I was with you except Jesus Christ and him crucified. I came
> to you in weakness and fear, and with much trembling. My
> message and my preaching were not with wise and per-
> suasive words, but with a demonstration of the Spirit's
> power, so that your faith might not rest on men's wisdom,
> but on God's power.
>
> 1 CORINTHIANS 2:1–5

The same could be true about our songs. They do not
need to be eloquent to communicate the gospel. They can
be simple yet true. They can be short and concise and reflect
the essence of the message.

It troubles me when people compare well-articulated
doctrinal hymns with simple choruses like As the Deer based
on Psalm 42. There is no need for comparison in that both
are true to the gospel in their own way. A song does not
need to have antiquated English to communicate the gospel
truth any more than a sermon needs to be infused with
King James quotes to be a good sermon. They just both
need to be true.

I am of the opinion that our criticism of music in the
church is, at best, lamentable. We are too busy wondering
whether we should sing hymns or contemporary choruses
(contemporary for the most part defined as music of the
sixties) while the potential for growth in all of the arts in
the church remains untapped. It is time for us to realize
that God loves all kinds of music and instrumentation

(read Psalm 150). The question is, does the text bring him glory and honor?

The text does not need to be complicated to be true. For words to be true, they just need to be true. They do not need to be grandiose. At the same time, they do not need to be overly simplified either. We just need to learn how to use words to communicate. If they communicate the truth of the gospel, then they have done their job.

Proclamation of the Scriptures

It is an understatement to say that the proclamation of the gospel is going to ultimately take place through the reading, teaching, and preaching of the Scriptures. Paul wrote to Timothy, "Until I come, devote yourself to the public reading of Scripture, to preaching and to teaching" (1 Tim. 4:13). There should be devotion to the Scriptures in our worship service. When people come to our churches, they should hear the Word of God.[3]

Some have expressed concern that the music segments in our services have been the preliminaries to the preaching of the Word. Music should play a greater role than entertainment; it should lead us into the presence of the heavenly Father. But I am concerned that the trend is going the other way. The preaching and teaching of the Word is becoming addendum material to the music. This must change if our churches are to be lighthouses in our communities.

In the ministry of the Word, the faith of the body of Christ is enhanced, for faith comes from hearing the message, and the message is heard through the word of Christ (see Rom. 10:17). We need to remain faithful to the reading, teaching, and preaching of the Word, for these are the most important forms of proclamation.

Reading the Word

Recently in my small group, we decided to study the Book of Hebrews. Our normal pattern is to look at one section at a time and discuss how it applies to us. Yet, our first night, I had us read the entire book, all thirteen chapters. It took us only thirty minutes at a normal reading speed. Many people in our group had never had that experience before. They were not used to hearing the Word read in its complete context. We discovered that many favorite verses surfaced but that we had the tendency to take them out of context. By reading the entire book out loud we understood the context. We realized that this was a book of exhortation in the midst of persecution, and we interpreted it much more accurately by hearing it read in its entirety.

Reading the Scriptures aloud whether privately or publicly is a wonderful way of proclaiming the gospel. Just read the Word and let the Holy Spirit do the rest. It is imperative that we read not only the Psalms, as wonderful as the Psalms are, but that we read all of the Word throughout the year. This will give our people a healthy diet of hearing the Bible.

Another way to read the Word aloud is through responsive readings. This is a powerful means of proclaiming the Word of the Lord. The traditional approach is to have the pastor or worship leader read and have the people respond. However, you could have the women and men alternate reading. You could also have different sections read, such as the east and west section. Especially powerful is incorporating a children's section in the responsive reading of the Scriptures.

Still another way to creatively read the Word is by having a readers' chorus or drama team read from different locations in the sanctuary. This unique way of reading the Word can truly enhance its impact. Constantly be thinking of new ways to proclaim the Scriptures through the reading of the Word.

Preaching and Teaching the Word

The next approach to proclaiming the Scriptures is through the preaching and teaching of the Word. Not only should the Word be read; it should also be explained. This is why God has given the gift of preaching and teaching in the body of Christ. He wants messengers who will not only declare the Word but also explain what it means. The preaching and teaching of the Word must be central in our worship.

As we preach and teach the Word in our services, we should proclaim Christ and his kingdom. It is through the Scriptures that we understand the God who has redeemed us. We need to realize that without the correct information on who God is, we will slip into idolatry. This is why our understanding of revelation and redemption is so imperative. Again, being a disciple of Jesus Christ means that we proclaim what we have seen and heard (see 1 John 1:3–4).

The pastor who is entrusted with the privilege of preaching and teaching the Word must do so with the understanding that it requires skill. In the same way a musician must practice to learn his or her instrument, the teacher of God's Word should study to better communicate that Word.

First, the teacher or preacher of the Word of God must focus on *content*. You may have heard it said that it does not matter what you say, just how you say it. For a teacher of God's Word, this is unacceptable. It matters both *what* you say and *how* you say it. You must teach the Word of God with credibility in your worship services.

When I speak of content, I am referring to the needed exegetical skills for preaching. The Word must be proclaimed with integrity as to its historical/cultural context and with grammatical, lexical, and theological accuracy.

As preachers and teachers of the Word, we must ask what a particular passage meant to the original audience. Then we must ask how it applies to our lives. Exegesis *does* matter. The teaching and preaching of the Word of God is crucial to proclamation in the worship service.

Not only is content important; *delivery* is equally important. We must learn *how* to teach and preach in such a way that we communicate with the people. The following areas regarding delivery are imperative: logical flow, big idea, eye contact, storytelling, being passionate, and asking for commitment.

As to logical flow, it might be easy to place this in the content category (certainly it does pertain to the content), yet if the logical flow is missing, it will greatly impact the delivery. Many times the impact in a sermon does not happen because the sermon does not make sense. A teacher and preacher of God's Word must think about form: introduction, body, conclusion, and transitions. Again, to use the musical analogy, a song has form. Most songs have an introduction, body, and conclusion along with the necessary transitions. A teacher of the Word must realize that lack of form is lack of order, which simply promotes confusion.

A big idea in the sermon will also enhance delivery; this is one of the reasons topical preaching is so powerful. If you give people a big idea they will be with you attentively throughout the sermon. If you give your people a dozen things to think about in your sermon, I guarantee they will forget what you preached the minute they leave the sanctuary.

The next area of delivery is eye contact; you *must* have eye contact with your people. If you want to proclaim the Word effectively through preaching and teaching, do not read your sermon; this is disastrous. I have yet to see an effective communicator who reads a manuscript. If I am sitting in the pew and the preacher is not looking at me or anyone else in the congregation, it communicates that this person does not care about the people to whom he or she is speaking. Just as eye contact is important in a personal one-on-one context, so it is important in a preaching and teaching context.

The ability to tell stories also helps the delivery of teaching. Jesus was a storyteller, and the people listened. They realized that he preached with authority unlike the scribes. Jesus came along and told stories about the Kingdom of God. If you have been entrusted with the privilege of teaching or preaching the Word, tell stories to help us understand the Story.

Furthermore, tell us stories that will help us commune with you and with our heavenly Father. Tell us about your life and how you have struggled to apply what you are preaching. Show us how the Father gave you victory over this situation. Eugene Peterson tells us that words can be used for two different purposes:

> In a kind of rough-and-ready sorting out, words can be put into two piles: words used for communication, and words used for communion. Words for communion are the words used to tell stories, to make love, nurture intimacies, develop trust. Words used for communication are used to buy stocks, sell cauliflower, direct traffic, teach algebra. Both piles of words are necessary, but words for communion are the pastor's specialty. If we approach people as masters of communication, we are as out of place as a whore at a wedding. We are not here to sell intimacy. We are here to be intimate. For that we use words of holy communion.[4]

This is important if you desire to effectively proclaim the Word of the Lord in the preaching or teaching context. You must let us in on a relationship not only with God but also with you. For me, some of the most unforgettable moments in the proclamation of the Word have been by people who shared not only the gospel but also their very lives (1 Thess. 2:8). This takes a certain amount of vulnerability and transparency. Let me assure you that people are trying to not only hear the gospel but also see how it is lived. In your stories, bring us into communion with you and with God.[5]

You must also be passionate about the Word of the Lord if you are to proclaim the gospel with effectiveness. The most effective teachers and preachers are simply men and women who are in love with Jesus and his Word. It comes across in their preaching and teaching. They are passionate in their relationship with Jesus and in their preaching of God's Word. Passion is a must if you desire to see your worship services ignite with revival.

Last of all, ask for commitment. The church needs to be mobilized, not just informed. Tell us specifically what to do and then ask us to do it. Jesus asked for commitment, and so did his disciples. Now we must do likewise. We cannot afford to proclaim the Word without asking for some kind of response; we must empower the body of Christ for action.

To preach and teach the Word is an awesome responsibility. Every Christian as a disciple has his or her responsibility to proclaim the Word, but the worship leader, whether musician or preacher, must faithfully know the content of the Word and be able to effectively proclaim it. This is a key element in the worship service, not addendum material. If the worship service is to remain faithful to the Lord, the preaching and teaching of the Word must have priority.

Reprise

Ultimately, the complete worship leader proclaims Christ; this is what distinguishes Christian worship from Islamic or Buddhist worship. We proclaim Christ and what he has done.

I was recently on vacation and had an opportunity to watch some programming on Christian television. The particular preachers I heard told me what I needed to do and how I had to live to please Christ. All of them were full of exhortation on what Christian living was to look like. Yet, none of them mentioned what Christ had done, is doing, or will do. To be honest with you, I could have turned on an info-mercial and listened to a motivational speaker and received the same message. When will we learn that the gospel is what Christ has done, is doing, and will do. Let us stop preaching ourselves and preach Jesus Christ as Lord (2 Cor. 4:5). Even when we are asking the people of God to do something, we need to remind them of the Spirit of God and his work in our lives. He has not asked us to play a solo but rather to join him in a duet.

Worship leaders are disciples of Jesus Christ who just cannot keep silent about Jesus. They constantly have to be telling people about his goodness and are persistently gossiping the gospel. They need to let people in on the message that salvation is possible through none other than Jesus Christ. This is what proclamation is about.

I have stated that there are many ways of proclaiming the Lord Jesus Christ. We proclaim the Lord in our behavior as worship leaders. We proclaim the Lord in our speech, in our songs, in our families. We proclaim the Lord in the preaching and teaching of his Word.

In the next section we are going to look at a specific way of proclaiming Christ: the arts. We are going to explore how to appreciate beauty and how to create beauty. This is a very special way that God has given us whereby we can communicate our love back to him.

PART THREE

BECOMING AN ARTIST

INTRODUCTION
TO PART THREE

Heart worship is enriched by the arts. A clear understanding must be gained that art will not give birth to true worship, but true worship will give birth to artistic expression. Art in every form can help us perceive the nature of God. His truth, His being, His attributes, His plan of redemption, His eternal program can all be visualized and realized through artistic expression to the intellect and emotion.[1]

Artists know how to appreciate and create. They are part of a creative process. They compose and create art because that is their calling. We will discuss these two themes, appreciation and creation, in the next two chapters. Complete worship leaders must not only be theologians and disciples but artists as well. They must have the ability to influence the worshiping congregation with the arts. They must be able to articulate, through their art form, the message that God reveals as he redeems a people for himself.

_____ *five* _____

APPRECIATION

THE COMPLETE WORSHIP LEADER must grow in the ability to appreciate beauty. I am assuming that the reader does believe that beauty does exist and that this is something objective. We will take up this discussion a bit more in this chapter. I am also assuming that the reader has the ability to intrinsically appreciate the good. We will discuss a foundation for aesthetics in this chapter. As a starting point for this discussion, let us turn to the Book of Genesis.

THE BOOK OF GENESIS AND APPRECIATION FOR BEAUTY

We are told in the very first book of the Bible, "In the beginning God created the heavens and the earth. . . . And God said, 'Let there be light,' and there was light" (Gen. 1:1, 3). God goes on to create the rest of the natural order, and after every creative act, the biblical text tells us *God saw that it was good* (Gen. 1:4, 10, 12, 18, 21, 25, 31). This phrase is repeated seven times in the first chapter of Genesis. The concluding verse in chapter one states, "God saw all that he had made, and it was very good" (Gen. 1:31).

God not only had *the ability* to appreciate what he created, he actually *did* appreciate it. He really enjoyed what he had created.

Since we are created in his image, we too have the ability to look at what God has created and declare with the Lord, "This is good." We can look at the natural order with amazement and conclude that it is impossible for God not to exist. It takes more faith to look at creation and declare that God does not exist than conclude that the only possible answer is God. What God has created is truly good.

What is it that makes it good? What is it that God saw and concluded that it was good? Did he declare that it was good because he created it or is there something special about what he created in and of itself? Is there something about the creative act or is it the end result that was good?

Order, Beauty, and Worship

One of the elements that makes beauty is order. When God created the universe, there was order in the sequence of created events. There was order in the division of opposites and functionality within each act. There was purpose in each distinctive part of creation. God did not just create elements with no function or purpose.

What makes the creation account fascinating is that God created the natural order without materials. There were no paintbrushes, colors, or canvases. When we create, we only rearrange elements that already exist, but when God created, he created out of nothing.

All of us have a built-in sense of order. We might not know how to articulate what we are feeling, but we know when something is in order and when it is not.

If you drive through a residential neighborhood and see one house with a manicured lawn, trimmed bushes, and fresh paint and later see another house with a weed-infested yard and chipped paint, it is easy to tell which house is more beautiful.

What makes the house with the manicured lawn more beautiful? It is the sense of order. The house that has been cared for is orderly. In contrast, the house that has not been cared for is disorderly. When there is an absence of order, there is a loss of beauty. When someone has not taken the time to organize, there is disruption. Order is the foundation of beauty.

Let us now apply this to our worship services. If the praise band gets up to lead in praise songs and the guitarist is playing wrong chords, there is disorder and dissonance. The congregation knows something is wrong. They might not know *what* is wrong, but they know that what they are hearing is not beautiful.

The same is true if the soloist sings half-a-pitch flat. Not only does the worshiper say that the solo is bad but that the worship experience is bad. Order is foundational to aesthetic appreciation.

Nobody knew this better than the apostle Paul. When addressing the church at Corinth, he pleaded for order. The body of Christ was not edified because of disorder:

> What then shall we say, brothers? When you come together, everyone has a hymn, or a word of instruction, a revelation, a tongue or an interpretation. All of these must be done for the strengthening of the church. If anyone speaks in a tongue, two—or at the most three—should speak, one at a time, and someone must interpret. If there is no interpreter, the speaker should keep quiet in the church and speak to himself and God.
>
> Two or three prophets should speak, and the others should weigh carefully what is said. And if a revelation comes to someone who is sitting down, the first speaker should stop. For you can all prophesy in turn so that everyone may be instructed and encouraged. The spirits of

prophets are subject to the control of prophets. For God is not a God of disorder but of peace.

1 CORINTHIANS 14:26–33

The result of an orderly worship service is a strengthened church. In a worship service members should not only praise the Lord, they should be edified as well. If the body of Christ is not being strengthened, the congregational worship service is the culprit.

The apostle Paul wanted each person to be heard and not get in the way of others. There is nothing more disorderly than everyone clashing because they will not listen to each other. The same principle is used in orchestration. Has it ever amazed you that in a professional orchestra, musicians get paid for not playing half the time? If you have ever been to a symphony concert, you know that the strings, woodwinds, brass, and percussion come in at the right time and they complement each other. Not everyone will be playing at the same time except when the score demands otherwise.

In an orchestra all have a part to play and, when it is not their turn, they do not play. The beauty of the body of Christ should be that, metaphorically, we hear the strings, woodwinds, brass, and percussion. There is order in spirit and function.

If you are leading a praise band in a worship service, make sure that everyone is not playing at the same time. For instance, in a slow worship chorus, have the piano or guitar give the introduction; then add a soloist. When you get to the chorus, add the praise team vocalist or choir and also the drums, bass guitar, and keyboards. However you arrange, do not let everyone play all the time. Teach your musicians the discipline of refraining from playing for the sake of listening to someone else.

By thinking through this issue of order, you will be adding a sense of beauty and creating a more edifying worship experience. By examining everything that is disorganized and fixing it, you will be able to plan a more cohesive service.

Take the area of preaching. When a sermon is disorganized in structure, hearers will find it hard to follow the preacher and to know what the sermon is about; this leads to frustrated worship because the hearers have no idea what is going on.

The same is true of the physical structure of the sanctuary. If a light bulb is burned out or if the sound system is squealing, worship will be interrupted. There will be something inside every individual that will declare this is not a beautiful situation. We need order to contribute to a worshipful experience. Understanding this relationship between order, beauty, and worship is imperative for the complete worship leader.

Is Beauty a Matter of Taste?

Is beauty a matter of one's personal taste? This question could be answered yes and no. Yes, it is true that people can adapt their taste to whatever they like. We would call this subjective preference. But every aesthetic judgment is not actually beautiful. One could be fascinated by a guitar playing out of tune. Many modern composers have made it their objective to portray disorder. But just because one develops such a taste does not make it objectively beautiful.

I have discovered that people's appreciation of art is inconsistent. Most people do have a sense of good and bad. They do have the ability to look for the best-looking house in the best-looking neighborhood for the amount of money their paycheck can afford. I am not speaking of accumulation but of appreciation.

I never appreciated orchestral music until I went to my first concert. After my fourth or fifth concert, I was convinced that this was beautiful music. How does one compare Mozart with Marilyn Manson? The answer is to experience both over a period of time. If one is at all honest, he or she will acknowledge that there is something objectively beautiful about the one and not the other. I can choose to love the less beautiful; people do it all the time. But there is no valid argument for which is the more objectively beautiful as with the cut lawn and the lawn with weeds.

As this pertains to church worship, your people might be used to poor music and preaching, but if they get the experience of good music and preaching somewhere else it will be difficult getting them back. You can complain about consumerism, but if you are not giving people the best, people will leave to find quality.

Are you honoring God by giving your best? Are you honoring him by working on the sermon, the music, and whatever else needs improvement? Let us strive to give our people the best music, the best preaching, the best drama—the best overall aesthetic experience—so that they can appreciate and participate in dynamic worship services that glorify the King of the universe.

Paul gave the church at Philippi good advice that could apply to aesthetics: "Finally, brothers, whatever is true, whatever is noble, whatever is right, whatever is pure, whatever is lovely, whatever is admirable—if anything is excellent or praiseworthy—think about such things" (Phil. 4:8). This should be our checklist.

First of all, is this true? The word *true* in Greek is the word *aleitheia,* meaning that which is truthful, real, honest, and genuine. Some music is written with no true content and no true context. Some people write songs to make money and to be popular. Why not write songs that express the genuineness of Christianity lived out in earthen vessels? Why not write songs that doctrinally capture Christianity? The songs of the complete worship leader must be truthful and genuine.

Second, is this noble *(semnos)?* Other translations use words like serious, of good character, honorable, worthy, respectable. Is this piece worth an award or is it something pulled together at the last minute? If it is not worth winning an award, it is not good enough for God or the people of God. There are some hymns that I refuse to sing because of the text and music. This is not a contemporary or traditional issue; it is an issue of musical integrity. We need to raise the overall standard.

Third, is this right *(dikaios)?* Does this music demonstrate the justice and righteousness of God? Here we enter into a moral category. Some art clearly perverts the righteousness of God. The Greek word *dikaiow* is directly linked to a right relationship with God.

Fourth, is this pure? This word is derived from the Greek word *agnos,* which means not only pure but holy, chaste, and innocent. Is this song reflective of moral purity or moral perversion? Does this song make me want to live a life of purity?

Fifth, is this lovely *(prospsileis)?* Is this pleasing or lovely? Some Christian music today is market driven, not aesthetically driven. Even though you have many people who enjoy and buy this music, some secular music is more lovely and pleasing.

Sixth, is this admirable *(eupsyeima)?* This word has the connotation that it is spoken well of by the people. The complete worship leader needs to care what the people think about the music selection. This requires a pastoral heart that is in tune with the culture of his or her congregation.

While I have applied Philippians 4:8 only to music, the same test should apply to every other part of the service. From the ushers and greeters to the preludes and postludes, the sermon, the offering, the announcements, the Lord's table, baptism, and every other element in the worship service, we should strive for excellence.

The higher we raise the standard on the quality of what we are doing, the more our worship services will be aesthetically enjoyable. It really is hard to appreciate an unprepared service. Someone might ask, What about spontaneity in a worship service? Let me answer as one who happens to be a jazz musician. Improvisation is the world of jazz music. Yet, improvisation is impossible without structure. Every great improviser knows the form, tune, and chords of a song and the appropriate scales to improvise within that chordal structure. This balance of form and spontaneity are found in other professions, such as standup comedy, acting, and playing baseball. Every time I lead worship, I purposely plan for moments of spontaneity. Yet, this is not synonymous with being unprepared. When something is nicely done, we appreciate the care that went into the project. So it is with our worship services. Let us give God our very best.

Becoming a Lover of Art

I love many styles of music and various expressions of art. Cultivated within me is the appreciation for beauty with all of the arts. I feel this love of art is important for worship leaders, for we must enjoy what we are doing, namely, appreciating and creating beauty.

There are many ways to do this. First, learn to appreciate many kinds of music by listening to a variety of styles and genres that are outside of what you normally listen to. Many people are surprised that I love Italian opera, especially Puccini, Verdi, and Rossini. I love this music because it is passionate; it is not synthetic or de-humanized. It presents all aspects of life, including human capriciousness. I also love to listen to Louis Armstrong, Miles Davis, and John Coltrane. These are my jazz heroes. Furthermore, I enjoy listening to well-crafted bands like Steely Dan, Los Lobos, and U2. Learning to appreciate great composers and different styles of music is beneficial and necessary for worship leaders.

Second, visit art museums, attend orchestra concerts, read great books, read poetry, peruse botanical gardens, look at the stars, and visit cathedrals, taking note of various forms of architecture. Enter the beauty that is all around you.

Third, if finances and time permit, travel to Europe. I have been fortunate to minister throughout the U.K., Scandinavia, and Europe. Three times I have led a team to the Czech Republic to teach English and share the gospel. What wonderful memories I have of Prague, the Charles Bridge, the Castle, and St. Vitus's Cathedral. A trip to Europe will help you learn to love and appreciate beauty in the arts.

USING THE FIVE SENSES TO APPRECIATE BEAUTY

Another way to appreciate beauty is to engage all five senses—hearing, sight, touch, smell, and taste—in the world of order. All of the senses must appreciate the goodness of the Lord and must be redeemed for the worship of God.

Worshiping with Hearing

We should train our ears to appreciate only the best of music whether contemporary or traditional. We should make it our goal to build a repertoire of only the best praise choruses, hymns, anthems, preludes, offertories, and postludes. Is the melody beautiful? Is the harmony beautiful? Does the rhythm complement the song? Does the song have enduring qualities?

This is not a hymn or chorus issue. There are some hymns that are poorly written melodically and harmonically, not to mention textually. We should not be concerned with the popularity of a hymn or chorus but whether it honors the Lord.

As with hymns, I will sometimes listen to a whole praise and worship CD and maybe choose one of the songs on that CD. The question I ask is not, Do I like this, but, Is this good? Does it have enduring qualities melodically, harmonically, rhythmically, and textually? Some people make their selection of goodness based only on the music. This is important, but it is only one of many factors.

To reiterate Buddy Owens' criteria, is it easy to learn, hard to forget, and scriptural? This guide is especially helpful for congregational worship. We also need to consider the participatory element, which we will look at in chapter 8. Singing *Messiah* by George Frideric Handel obviously meets all of the aesthetic standards, but it is not practical for most congregations to sing.

There are some simple hymns and choruses ("Amazing Grace" and "Lord, I Lift Your Name on High," for example) that are easy to learn and have enduring qualities: the melody is singable and enjoyable; the harmony complements the melody; the rhythm supports the melody instead of competing against it; and the text is biblical and creedal.

The same evaluations must be made about Scripture readings, sermons, and announcements. We must provide beauty for the sense of hearing; we cannot be complacent. Excellence is something we must constantly strive for.

Every pastor could benefit from voice lessons. We have had homiletics courses that focused on the technicalities of putting a sermon together, yet maybe what we need to work on is voice projection, diction, variation, voice tone, and quality. It is probable that your worship pastor or minister of music spent years developing his or her voice. As a senior pastor, try to give attention to the development of the voice as well.

Worshiping with Sight

What do people see when they come into our sanctuary? Is it orderly? Is it beautiful? Are the chairs or pews cleaned? Are the pulpit, communion table, and platform arranged? Is the pulpit chipped? Does the piano have scratches on it? Does the color scheme contribute to worship? Does the color of the walls complement the carpeting? Are the words and symbols on the banners understandable? Is there clutter in your worship center? Can the people read the PowerPoint presentation? Do you have plants and other greenery to give a sense of life?

These kinds of questions are imperative for worship leaders. If there is distraction when people come to the service, the worship experience will suffer. Clothing is also a part of the visual arts. I have been in churches where the choir members wore robes and in other churches where they did not. This is not a contemporary or traditional issue but a matter of being orderly. Whether your church is more progressive or traditional in dress style, make sure you and your musicians always look sharp on the platform.

Worshiping with Touch

There are many creative ways of engaging touch when worshiping together. One way is to have a place in your worship service where the body of Christ joins hands and prays together. Another way of worshiping with the touch is your greeting time. Have people shake someone else's hand or give a hug if they know the person well enough. By having a time of greeting, passing the peace, and giving the worshipers opportunity to embrace each other, you will be providing appreciation through the touch.

Another way of engaging this kind of worship is to have people clap their hands on faster songs. This adds to the excitement in praise songs and engages the body of Christ in worshiping with their physical bodies.

One last way of experiencing worship with the touch is with baptism. When you are baptized, you are declaring that your old nature is being buried with Christ and that you are taking on a new nature. I can still remember the day I baptized my oldest son. It was a glorious worship experience for both of us. There was something very powerful about being in the water together and my son articulating his faith in Christ. Whether individuals are baptized as infants, older children, or adults, every baptism is cause for rejoicing. It is another way of celebrating what Christ has done for us.

Engaging the Sense of Smell

Regarding the sense of smell, many Orthodox churches have something to teach us. They effectively engage the sense of smell in their worship by using incense and scented candles. In non-Orthodox churches, this same effect can be accomplished by fresh cut flowers or by a pleasant air freshener. Yet, you must be sensitive to those who are allergic to such scents.

When using scented candles, the smell should be pleasant, not overbearing. If it is too dominant, you will be focusing on the scent instead of the worship experience. In our church, the janitor puts a nice fragrance in the cleaner when he vacuums. The principle that I like to use is, how would you like your house to smell if you were to invite guests? This is the same question you should ask if you have the intention of inviting guests into your church. Provide a pleasant scent that will enhance the worship experience.

When celebrating Advent and Christmas, use a spiced apple potpourri and provide spiced cider at your information table. This will give a wonderful scent during this season. Think about how to match the scent to the occasion.

Engaging the Sense of Taste

Concerning the sense of taste in a worship experience, the best place for this is during a communion service. Many times I have forgotten a sermon I heard but always remembered partaking of communion. There are creative ways of making the environment of the Lord's table special. For example, in a recent communion service I led, we baked bread prior to the worship service. Both the smell and the taste of fresh-baked bread made the service special.

I really do believe we have underestimated the importance of communion in our evangelical churches. This is a wonderful way of celebrating the Lord and his death and of engaging the sense of taste in the experience.

REPRISE

There are many ways to engage the five senses in the worship experience, but we must explore with good judgment and not do anything inappropriate. We need to learn how to worship the Lord with everything that is within us. We need to realize the importance of the arts in our worship services. Appreciation of beauty is a wonderful thing, and beauty has to do with order, whether it be arranging a piece of music, a sermon, or the color scheme in the sanctuary. May we honor the Lord by appreciating beauty.

The next time you see something that is beautiful, analyze the areas of order. Compare what is orderly about the artwork and how this makes it beautiful. Apply this test the next time you purchase a worship CD.

As worship leaders, we need to distinguish great works of art from average art. We need to begin to expose our churches to great art whether pre-composed or self-composed. God deserves our best!

CREATION

IN CHAPTER 5, I proposed that an artist must have the ability to appreciate beauty. This is the starting point for the artist. If the artist cannot articulate what constitutes good art, then creating art will be difficult.

In this chapter we will look at three philosophical approaches to creating art: formalism, expressionism, and referentialism. The formalistic view states that the technical aspects of art need to be emphasized. The expressionistic view states that the emotional aspects of art need to be emphasized. The referentialistic view states that all art has a reference point and that this needs to be emphasized. Each one of these approaches to creating art is equally important; they depend upon each other. I will specifically discuss the three philosophical approaches as they apply to music.

FORMALISM

Formalism is like the foundation of a house; without the foundation, building the remaining structure is impossible. We have all experienced a situation where someone was playing out of tune. Because of this formalistic issue (into-nation), our worship experience was diverted from Christ to tuning problems. Bennet Reimer states, "The study of art as a 'discipline,' with primary attention given to the accu-mulation of information or the development of skills, is for-malistic in flavor."[1] The development of fundamental skills is imperative for the artist. The musician must master notes, scales, chords, and rhythms. The preacher must work on sentence structure, logic, and delivery. The key term is *skill*. The formalist is interested in the acquisition of skill.

The Importance of Skill

Cultivating skill will enable us to express ourselves as artists. A musician who cannot play his or her instrument will be impaired when it comes to expression. The same is true for pastors who are under the impression that their personalities will make them great communicators. The preacher must learn exegetical skills, logic, and delivery technique.

For each skill to be learned, there are certain laws that God has created that make that skill work. If you are going to be a writer, you must learn how to put words together. If you are going to be a musician, you must learn how notes and scales work. If you are going to be a communicator, you must learn the laws of communication. There are no shortcuts when it comes to learning the basics. The for-malist is concerned with the development of these basic skills. Therefore, to become a complete worship leader, you must become a formalist.

The Importance of Details

Details are important to the formalist. For the choir director, for instance, one tenor singing wrong notes is unacceptable even if all the other tenors are singing the right notes. Allen and Borror give us an illustration concerning the importance of details:

> The story is told of a craftsman who had traveled to America from Europe to dedicate his life to some of the detail work of one of this country's grandest places of worship. One day a sightseer was touring the edifice and observed the workman meticulously laboring near the high ceiling on a symbol which could hardly be seen from the floor. What is more, he seemed to be occupied with a detail on the top, even out of view of the most carefully observant worshiper. The sightseer said, "Why are you being so exact; no one can even see the detail you are creating from this distance?" The busy artist replied, not missing a stroke, "God can!"[2]

One of the issues a formalist will not tolerate is sloppiness. An artist is first and foremost a perfectionist about formalistic considerations. God deserves our best. Again, Allen and Borror are helpful: "We are not to offer to God that which costs nothing. Why do we give Him our junk pianos, old clothes, shabby buildings, poorly prepared music, half-ready sermons, last minute Sunday school lessons."[3] The worship leader who desires to give God the best will be the worship leader who leads the people of God into a dynamic experience in God's presence.

Because most worship leaders are musicians, I will give musical examples and suggestions throughout the rest of this chapter. If you are not a musician, look at these examples and ask which elements pertain to your particular art form.

Formalistic Musical Concerns

The following considerations are formalistic: correct intervals, correct rhythms, intonation, harmony, melody, entrances, cutoffs, diction, articulation, key signatures, time signatures, and blend. I will offer suggestions for rehearsal and performance as we look at each of these issues.

Correct Intervals

Pitch is determined by the number of vibrations per second; this is also known as frequency. Intervals on the other hand have to do with the relationship between one pitch and another. When we say "that person is singing or playing the wrong notes" we mean the relationship between one pitch and another pitch is not right. Maybe the musician is not playing in the correct key signature. It is at this point that we must determine what is causing one to be playing or singing the "wrong" notes.

To practice intervals, it is beneficial to learn all the key signatures and the notes that are within those keys. For example, the key of F contains one flat (b flat). Therefore, your notes in the key of F will be: f, g, a, b flat, c, d, e, f. The second suggestion is to look for accidentals (notes that are not in the key you are performing in) and determine if they match the harmony (chordal changes) or if they are just passing notes.

Vocalist. If you are a vocalist, (1) isolate the text and sing your notes on *LA* to focus on the interval. By doing so, you are eliminating the added burden of singing the correct words. (2) Work with a piano so that you are playing the correct intervals. (3) Work the troubled area slowly, giving your ear time to hear the intervals. (4) Record yourself with a tape player. What you hear in your head and what the audience hears are usually different.

Vocalist with instrumentalists. If you are working with a vocalist combined with instrumentalists, isolate one or the other. It is impossible to try to work on correct notes if everyone is performing at the same time. I have seen numerous situations where this has been a problem. At some point, you must determine what your rehearsal is to look like.

Instrumentalist. Do not be too concerned with everything at once. Work on what you need to work on. You need not worry about dynamics or other nonformalistic concerns at this point. Get the notes right. Use the second through fourth principles for vocalist.

Correct Rhythms

Rhythm is sound in space and time. "Blurry" rhythms reveal an amateur musician quicker than anything else. As a young trumpet player, I was a very impatient musician. I thought that the key to being a great trumpet player was to play high, fast, and loud. The problem was that I played incorrect rhythms because I did not have the patience to slow down. This is like the downhill skier who wants to get down the mountain as fast as possible but in the process runs into a tree or other skiers.

Take the time to sing or play the correct rhythms. Every time you practice something incorrectly, it will become more difficult to correct the problem. The following suggestions will help you improve in this area.

If you are a vocalist, say your words in tempo. Do not worry about singing the right notes; focus on the correct rhythms. I have done this many times with choirs. Difficult sections are solved when you isolate the music and say the words.

If you are a vocalist or an instrumentalist, clap the correct rhythms. Incorrect rhythms occur when tempos are too fast. Slow the tempo down and beat out the correct rhythm.

Learn to subdivide. Subdividing is an issue of division. This depends on the tempo of the song and the main unit being used in the song. If I am singing "Amazing Grace," I want to subdivide eighth notes. This is the smallest unit used in this hymn. Other than the dotted half note tied to the half note at the end of each phrase, the largest unit is a half note. If I am only thinking about quarter notes (the main unit in 3/4 time) the tempo is bound to fluctuate. For more information on subdivision, consult the appendix.

Work with a metronome. Use an electronic metronome such as Dr. Beat, which can be plugged into a sound system. This helps identify the sections that are speeding up or slowing down. The other benefit of a metronome like Dr. Beat is that the subdivisions are accessible. For example, indicate on the metronome that you want to emphasize the eighth notes. This subdivision will be heard through the sound system.

Intonation

Intonation is crucial for the formalist and can be defined as singing or playing in tune. Intonation is derived from listening, technical facility, and a workable instrument. Non-musicians can identify this category the most quickly. They can tell if you are out of tune. The following are suggestions for improving intonation.

Spend time developing your ear with various ear-training exercises. You do this by interval association. A tritone upward sounds like "Maria" from *West Side Story.* A minor 2nd upward sounds like the theme from *Jaws.* A perfect 4th upward sounds like "Here Comes the Bride." A perfect 5th upward sounds like "Twinkle, Twinkle, Little Star." A major 6th upward sounds like the NBC theme. A minor 3rd upward sounds like "Greensleeves." A major 2nd upward sounds like "Happy Birthday to You." A minor 3rd downward sounds like "Hey Jude." Spend time listening to each interval and associate a tune with that interval. This will enhance your intonation.

Work on problems slowly and repetitively. The following will contribute to poor vocal intonation: inappropriate diaphragmatic-costal breathing, over-singing, the incorrect placement of the tongue (you should keep your tongue behind your bottom teeth on all of your vowels), and shifting from the chest voice to head voice (passagio). Again, work with a piano and tape recorder. Sing the passage using only vowels. Then add the consonants.

If you are an instrumentalist, isolate all factors and figure out what is wrong. The problem could be a physiological one (not supporting a brass or woodwind instrument adequately), a mechanical one (not tuning your instrument with an A440 tuned piano), or sloppy delivery (not working the passage slowly). Work with a piano, a tuner, and a tape recorder.

Correct Harmony and Melody

What is the difference between harmony and melody? Harmony is the chordal or vertical structure of a piece of music; melody is the horizontal structure. When a composer writes music in which the melody complements a song, this is consonance. When a melody is written to clash against the harmony, this is dissonance. The key is that dissonance is intentional. Unintentional dissonance probably means that you are playing something incorrectly. You must determine what is wrong. The following suggestions will help you avoid unnecessary angst.

Always work with a pianist and check the melody against the harmony. Know the intentional chordal change and not just the voicing. It might be that the composer meant the melody to supplement the intentional missing element in the harmony. When working with a band, make sure everyone has the same set of changes. Take time to check these details; this eliminates wasted time in the studio or rehearsal.

Think like a conductor. Know all the parts, not just your own. Know how you fit into the whole. If you are a vocalist and you sing tenor, learn the bass and alto lines. This is helpful if you need to cover someone else's part due to a sickness. Everybody should know the melody. For leading congregational singing, a rule of thumb is to always double the melody when adding a harmony part. This reinforces the melody, which assists the people to hear so that they can sing confidently.

Entrances and Cutoffs

Vocalists and instrumentalists sound sloppy when there is disagreement on entrances and cutoffs. Develop a system of dashes (or something similar, such as check marks) and have all the musicians mark the same notations in their music.

With this system, mark the dash and the beat you want something cut off on. For example, –3 means to cut that note off on beat three; –1 means to carry that note over to the beginning of the next measure and then cut it off. Once again, do not assume that people are going to know this intuitively. Do it together! Sloppy cutoffs usually contribute to sloppy entrances. Cutting a phrase off too soon or too late means that you will not come in on your next entrance with precision.

Diction and Articulation

Concerning diction and articulation, clarity is the key word. If you are singing a song and the message is important, help us understand the words. You must work on your diction. This problem will occur more frequently as you add more vocalists. I always tell my choirs to chew on the words. I want to see their mouths moving. Vocalists often fail to communicate because they do not appropriate the necessary diction.

Explode the consonants for great diction. Consonants are formed five different ways: (1) with the lips (B's, F's, M's, P's, and V's); (2) by the tongue and the teeth (D's, J's, T's, and TH's); (3) with the tongue (L's); (4) with the teeth (C's, S's, and Z's); and (5) in the throat (C's, K's, Q's, and G's). After you discover which part of the mouth is forming the consonant, overemphasize that consonant. For some articulation exercises, consult the appendix on tongue twisters.

For instrumentalists, articulation refers to the combination of slurs and attacks. For attacks, the key is what a player does at the beginning of a note. Brass players might need to appropriate more attack. My trumpet teacher at UNC, Bill Pfund, used to suggest playing a note with more tongue. By striking the note with more tongue, there was more clarity. Record yourself. If you cannot understand what you are singing or playing, it is probable that the audience will not be able to either.

This passage from Philip Farkas's *The Art of Musicianship* reinforces the importance of articulation marks in music:

> I believe it is inexcusable for the performer to disregard these articulation marks put into the music by the composer himself. Yet this oversight, or worse yet, disregard, for the composer's explicit articulation instructions is so common that I would consider it one of the most glaring faults of music students—or sadder yet—of many professionals, who should know better. Certainly we should respect the composer and his intentions. If we do not, we should at least have the courtesy to not perform his music.[4]

Correct Key Signatures and Time Signatures

Knowing your key signatures and time signatures is very important when sight reading. First check the key signatures; look for modulations or accidentals within the key signature that you are performing in. Then check the time signatures; look over the music for changes and mixed meters.

Blend

The next area of concern to the formalist is blend. When speaking of blend in music, we are asking what sounds nice together. The one element that kills group blend is individuality. When everyone wants to sing or play like a soloist there will be problems. When we start singing or playing *in community* we will achieve the desired sound. Therefore blend starts with our attitudes. We must listen to what is going on around us and then figure out how we fit into that sound. Following are some suggestions.

Vocal blend. The process I would go through in developing *vocal* blend would be: First of all, are we over-singing? Second, are we matching vowels? Third, are we singing with different vibratos? Fourth, are we striving to have the same tone placements? Is one person singing in the back of the throat and the other at the roof of the mouth? Fifth, do we need to change the voicings? This is a compositional consideration. Sixth, are we holding the microphones the same way? Seventh, what is the mix like at the sound board? Does one channel have lots of midrange and the other lots of bass? Are vocal channels similarly mixed only to be adjusted slightly for vocal differentiations? Blend should happen from the vocalist and not the sound technician. The sound system should only amplify what is being produced on the stage. Eighth, what is the monitor level like? The best monitor system is the simplest one (uncomplicated). If you have every instrument coming through the system you will need to process more information. On the other hand, if you have only the piano tuned to A440 coming through, for pitch reference, you will be much better off. You do not need every vocalist in a choir coming through the monitor system. When I was directing Continentals, we would only put the piano, director's mike, and solo mike through the vocal monitors. Vocalists need to learn to sing by feel.

Instrumental blend. Listening to what is going on around you is the key. Do not be so consumed with your own musical part that you forget you are part of a group. Remember what role you are playing. A drummer and bass player need to remember that they are the foundation of rhythm. The bass player will usually be listening to what the drummer's kick drum is doing and vice versa. If you are the pianist in an ensemble, your function will primarily be harmonic in nature. It is imperative that you know various voicings and where to appropriately use them. If you are a brass or woodwind player, you will be there for fills, color, and solos. It is always important to define roles. If you are on a baseball team, only one person can bat at a time. If you have two pitchers, three batters, and no catcher simultaneously, you will not have baseball but chaos. Take the time to discuss who is establishing the rhythm, harmony, and melody. Your sound will have a much better blend as the result of honestly discussing who is responsible for what part.

Summary of Formalism

Whatever discipline we choose, we always have to get back to the basics. Formalistic considerations are the basics of art, and we must strive to perfect these areas. Again, this is the foundation. If we do not work on these areas, it is doubtful that we will succeed at the next two categories. They are dependent on the previous formalistic considerations. We should rehearse the technical aspects of music so many times that the technical subtleties eventually become automatic. This then frees us up to move on to the emotional aspects of music.

EXPRESSIONISM

If the formalistic view is the foundation, the expressionistic view is the paint, trimming, and decoration; this is what gives music beauty. An artist must have a canvas to paint on *and* the paint to put on the canvas; this is the emotional aspect of music. "Expressionists do not agree with formalists that the experience is an intellectual one. The expressionist part of the position connects the experience of art with feeling."[5] Whereas the concerns in the formalistic view were technical in nature, the expressionist will focus on what makes music emotional.

Expressionistic Musical Areas

An expressionist focuses on dynamics, phrasing, interpretation, body language, correct tempos, and expression marks. Each of these areas creates emotion.

Dynamics

For the expressionist, dynamics are important. Dynamics consider various degrees of volume. The question is, how are we contrasting loudness and quietness to create emotion? Music is tension and release. We have all sat through a movie and knew something was about to happen because of what the music was doing. We can create emotion if we put care into dynamics. Following are some guidelines.

In contemporary praise music, know where the chorus is and where the verses are. Crescendo into the chorus and decrescendo into the verses. The chorus is the message of the song. The verse tells us about the message but is usually not the message itself. Frequently the verse will ask a question and the chorus will give the answer. The verse will create a dilemma and the chorus will give us the solution. You must understand the composer. Know the message and communicate it dynamically.

Know the key changes. Key changes help to eliminate redundancy and give an additional dynamic lift to the previous section. Do not defeat this purpose by singing at one volume. Crescendo into key changes. Exceptions will be marked by the composer.

Know the entrances and endings. Start strong and end strong. If you are performing a quiet piece, set up the emotion of the song by entering and ending with boldness. Eradicate timidity in entrances and endings. People remember the first and last things they hear. When you perform at a quiet dynamic level, put in twice as much energy with diction and articulation to create the same force.

Have instrumentalists accentuate the kicks and punches.
Bring these out. They were written to fill a gap where no
singing is taking place. If you are backing up vocalists, the
message of the song is the important element in communication. Support the singer; do not compete. Competing
reveals a lack of musicianship and of character. When there
is no singing going on, bring out your part. Bring out intro-
ductions, endings, and punches.

*Check that everyone is appropriating the necessary dynam-
ics in the same spot.* Use a pencil. Dynamics are relative. Listen to some advice by Philip Farkas:

> No dynamic is limited to only one exact volume. Consider
> each dynamic as a sidewalk not as a tight-rope. This side-
> walk, though not very wide, is wide enough so that the
> dynamics can wander from one side to the other. In other
> words, each dynamic level has some rise and fall within
> itself—it is not restricted to a narrow line. This rise and fall
> is felt by the musician and used with discretion. It should
> not overlap into the next dynamic level in either direction,
> but certainly it can rise or fall within itself. Piano, mezzo
> forte and forte are relative to each other and have no exact
> value. I presume that an artillery soldier would consider the
> sound of his cannon to be fortissimo—until he heard an
> atomic blast—at which time he would be forced to admit
> that his cannon was pianissimo—relatively speaking.[6]

Be flexible and know how to adjust. The following will
determine dynamics: the importance of the passage, tone
color desired, size of the ensemble, size of the auditorium,
and your role in the group. Number your dynamic range
from 1 to 10. Practice everything at a 10 (forte), then 8, then
6, then 4, then 2 (piano).

In decrescendos, get rid of the note slowly. Articulate the
note, establish the note, then decrescendo. Extend your
dynamic range to both extremes. Use moderation 90 per-
cent of the time, keeping extreme ends of the dynamic

range in reserve for those moments when they will be effective. But have them available. Last of all, when playing a solo, be a little "too loud." When playing an accompaniment, play a little "too soft."[7]

Phrasing

The next area of importance for the expressionist is phrasing. The *Harvard Dictionary of Music* tells us that "A phrase is the division of a musical line, somewhat comparable to a clause or a sentence in prose."[8] How you shape phrases determines the energy and direction of the melodic line. If you are not thinking about phrasing, you will communicate boredom. As with dynamics, the key is tension and release. The phrase needs to have a beginning, a climax or pivot point, and an ending. Sometimes the climax is the ending. It is your responsibility to know where the climax or pivot point is. Give shape to the phrase. Philip Farkas states: "Karl Krueger, the articulate conductor of the Kansas City Philharmonic during my early symphony days, was fond of saying that a musical phrase lived. And, if it lived, it breathed. . . . The important thing, in this analogy of breathing to phrasing, is the feeling of mounting tension during inhalation and the gradual relaxation during exhalation."[9] The following suggestions will help you make phrases come alive.

Create the phrase with breath control. Your phrase needs to end where your breath ends. Time the necessary phrase and make sure it has a definitive ending. Do not exhaust yourself at the ends of phrases. Remember that giving direction to the phrase is directly correlated to dynamics. You need to crescendo toward your climax and diminuendo away from it.

The best way to determine a logical phrase is to say the words. Where would you put a period or a question mark? Where are the sentences within the song? Do not break up your sentences to take a breath. Complete the sentence, then take a breath. Exceptions would always be stylistic.

Give emphasis to words that communicate a certain mood. For example, in the hymn *Amazing Grace,* the words state, "Amazing grace, how sweet the sound, that saved a wretch like me." In singing this hymn, I would climax to "grace" in that this is what this hymn is about. I would emphasize the word "sweet" sweetly. I would emphasize "wretch" in that the message of salvation is for wretches like me. Figure out what words within the sentence are crucial and put special emphasis on them.

> Occasionally the pivot point is located at the highest pitched note in the phrase, although this is certainly not a definite criterion. Sometimes we find this point of maximum tension in a "suspension" note just before the resolution of the phrase. Whether your judgment agrees with that of other musicians or even whether you have chosen the very best pivot point is not as important as the fact that you have chosen a pivot point in the phrase. At least your phrase will be going somewhere—and having got there—will start to relax. It will breathe. Give life to those phrases.[10]

Another aid to the rise and fall in a phrase is the use of accelerando to the pivot point and ritardando away from it.[11] This suggestion has to do with the alteration of tempos to create tension. This is certainly a powerful way of creating emotion.

The bar line in music is one of the surest indicators of phrasing emphasis the composer can give us.[12] Usually the bar line indicates the end of a section. Work the section dynamically toward that line to create the phrase.

A change in tone color or an intensification of tone quality to approach the pivot-point and a gradual lightening of the tone as the phrase relaxes can be used effectively.[13] If you can execute tonal coloring, your artistic ability will really be transparent. This is a very creative way of shaping the phrase.

Interpretation

The next area of importance for the expressionist is interpretation, which has to do with the style of music you are singing. If you are singing a jazz piece, you need to emphasize the offbeats. 1 **AND** 2 **AND** 3 **AND** 4 **AND**. On each of the **ANDS**, I would put an accent (>) over the top of the note to give a swing to the eighth notes. This is interpretation.

Another example of interpretation is ornamentation. Ornamentation is the embellishment, usually containing additional notes in the melodic line, to spice up the music. The execution of ornamentation requires musical skill and knowledge of history. Ornamentation needs to be interpreted within the appropriate musical period. You must know the intent of the composer. If you were interpreting a foreign language, you would need a solid vocabulary and a knowledge of the intent of the message to be able to communicate the words and the message.

Ask historical and background questions about the composer. In what era was this written? Is this piece from the Renaissance, the Baroque, the Classical, the Romantic, the twentieth century? Is this a jazz piece? If it is, what style within the jazz idiom does this fall under (blues, ragtime, swing, bebop, cool jazz, avant garde, or fusion)? If the classification of this music is sacred, was this piece written for a cathedral with an organ or was it written during the Jesus Movement when the guitar was the primary instrument? If I am singing a chorus such as *In His Time,* I will use instruments like the acoustic guitar or flute. If I am singing *A Mighty Fortress Is Our God,* I will use an organist. Determine what instrumentation you need to re-create the setting in which the piece was written.

Body Language

Next on the list of expressionistic considerations is body language. I insert this category, even though it would fall under the visual arts, in that it does affect musical performance. In a video generation, people will hear what they see. Do you convince people that you mean what you are singing or playing? What you do with your body will dictate the emotion you communicate. This is important for vocalists in that you are not only communicating music but a message. Overdoing is like underdoing it. Our tendency is to be stiff and rigid. The best way to improve this area is to videotape yourself and work in front of a mirror. Especially when it comes to facial expressions, a mirror will help greatly.

Correct Tempos

In one sense the use of tempos is a formalistic consideration. Yet in another sense, tempos communicate emotion: boredom, excitement, anxiety, and so forth. Conductors must be very cautious in choosing tempos. Philip Farkas states, "How frustrating it is to rehearse with a conductor (sometimes a world-famous one) who fusses about the slightest detail: 'a little longer on this note,' 'a touch less accent,' 'a tiny ritardando here,' until these details are perfect, only to have him conduct a two-hour concert—all at the wrong tempos!"[14]

Listen to various recordings of the piece you are performing and determine the appropriate tempo for your situation. This is an interpretive judgment. The real question is, how accurate is your judgment? If your tempo choice is off you will lose the "groove." Remember that many people have struggled in the studio to find an accurate tempo that communicates the necessary emotion.

Know your music terminology. Below is a list of tempos and the appropriate musical term. Use these terms when writing in your music.

Grave	very, very slow, solemn, heavy, dragging
Largo	very slow, broad, stately
Adagio	slow, tranquil
Lento	slow
Andante	walking tempo, moving, going along
Andantino	a little faster than andante
Moderato	moderate
Allegretto	moderately fast
Allegro	fast, brisk, lively
Vivace	lively
Presto	very fast
Prestissimo	very, very fast

Become familiar with your metronome. Yet remember that the metronome "acts only as a clue, and a good musician uses the metronome simply as a guide to determine the average tempo in either direction, as his feeling for the music dictates."[15] One last suggestion would be to memorize various metronome markings by associating tunes with each marking.

Expression Marks

Become familiar with various expression marks such as accents, staccato marks, sostenuto marks, various articulations, fermatas, ritards, stringendos, and rubatos. Have a small pocket musical terms dictionary with you at all times. It helps to write in your music the translations of foreign terms until you eventually memorize them.

Artur Rodzinski, the late conductor of the Cleveland Symphony Orchestra, used to occasionally accuse a player of "missing a note." The player might retort, "No, sir, I played a B flat, just as written." Whereupon Rodzinski would reply, "You didn't play the accent!" In his mind a musical note was made up of several elements—pitch and rhythm, to be sure. But also volume, accent or non-accent, staccato or tenuto. And, if any one of these elements was left out, the note, in his belief, was missed! A belief well worth adopting. . . . Here is an old anecdote which might help illustrate how important all the elements of even one musical note can be: A trumpet player in the village band had just one solo to play in a certain composition. It consisted of one glorious golden note, played just right. But, at the performance, in his nervousness, the trumpeter made seven mistakes on his one note! He came in a measure too soon—he played the wrong note—the wrong note was too flat, even for the wrong note—the attack was too loud—the note made a crescendo instead of a diminuendo—the tone was fuzzy—and he held the note one measure too long![16]

Summary of Expressionism

Spend time working on the elements that make art emotional. The option is boring music. This is like the preacher who has the theology and sermon perfect. The only thing missing is conviction and passion. It is not enough to work on the technicalities of art. If we are serious about communication, we must bring out the emotion. After bringing out the emotion, we must be connected to the purpose of this art. This leads us to the third category, referentialism.

REFERENTIALISM

This third philosophical view simply states that all art has a reference point. When a composer is writing a piece of music, he or she has something in mind. When a painter is painting a picture, the artist has something in mind. There is a reference point. For us as worship leaders, the reference point is Jesus Christ and the Kingdom of God. We are connecting people to God.

To illustrate this, many televisions have picture in picture. You can watch two programs at the same time—one in the small box and the other in the big box. For human beings, there are three stories going on at all times: our personal story, the cultural story, and the Kingdom of God story. For the unchurched, they cannot see the Kingdom of God story, only the personal and cultural story. For the church, the Kingdom of God story is frequently the picture in the little box, and the personal or cultural story is the big picture. The purpose of worship is to reverse this. The Kingdom of God story should become the big picture and our personal and cultural story the little picture.[17] This is what a referentialist is thinking about. How can I as a worship leader help people see Jesus and the Kingdom of God? This is referentialism.

Referentialistic Musical Areas

The areas a referentialist will focus on are intent, appropriateness, and other issues of communication. These are essential to think about as we examine the reference point of music.

Intent

When we speak of intent, we are asking why this music was written. Was it written to speak of a historical event? Was it intended for a celebration or a time of sorrow? If I am performing a song for Easter, there will be a sense of celebration in remembrance of the resurrection. If I am performing a psalm of praise such as Psalm 103 there will be a sense of gratefulness and praise. If I am performing a requiem, there will be a somberness about the piece. The following are some suggestions that will help you determine the intent of the piece.

If the music has a text, study it and ask the same question you would of a book: What is the theme or big idea? What is this work all about? How is this theme communicated through the verses? What choice of words does the composer use? What is the original intent? *Do a cultural and historical analysis of the music and composer.* When was this written? What were the circumstances involved when it was written? Who was the composer? What were the circumstances of the composer? A great example of this would be many of our hymn composers. Many of the hymns were written during a difficult situation that the writer faced. I'm reminded of the great hymn "It Is Well with My Soul." It is speculated that Horatio G. Spafford penned the words of this hymn after joining his bereaved wife following the sinking of an English vessel where they lost their four daughters. In trying to understand those circumstances, we will communicate the song more effectively.

Appropriateness

Next, the referentialist will be interested in the appropriateness of the music. This is similar to intent but different. Intent focuses on the composer's desire. Appropriateness focuses on discretionary decisions on our part. For example, in a communion service, would you use an upbeat song? Although we would all approach communion differently, there are musical pieces that would be inappropriate, in any church, for this important event. Is the music appropriate? There are seasons when we are asked to create music for an event. We must determine if our song selection will be appropriate. If I am choosing music for a communion service, I will reference the death of our Lord. Go back to the event and choose music that is appropriate.

Issues of Communication

Referentialists would also be interested in the theory of communication. They would ask whether one is communicating the message. There are many practical ways to improve our communication skills.

The principles of interpersonal communication apply for the musician. Nonverbal communication, tone of voice, and the actual content of the words are all part of communication. Is the audience bored or excited? You must know how to follow the body language of your audience. If they are falling asleep, figure out how to become a better communicator.

First, videotape yourself. Second, use an audiotape to record yourself. Third, establish people in your audience who can be honest and give you objective feedback. Fourth, design an evaluation form that has the various areas that you want to see covered. Give this to the people who will be critiquing you. They will then know what they should be looking for. And last, always remain teachable. Someone who knows it all will repeatedly fail as a worship leader. "God is opposed to the proud but gives grace to the humble" (1 Peter 5:5 NASB).

Summary of Referentialism

As we desire to be more effective communicators we will focus on the reference point of our music. What are we singing about? Who are we singing to? What do want to communicate? How do we want people to respond as an indicator that we are accomplishing our goal? All of these questions must be asked by the worship leader. The people who are the most effective in any field are the best communicators. May we strive to be not only excellent musicians but excellent in communication.

As Christians, we have the ultimate reference point. Our reference point is not ourselves, not our art, not our eloquence but God himself. In *Worship Is a Verb* Robert Webber says: "The focus of worship is not human experience, not a lecture, not entertainment, but Jesus Christ—his life, death, and resurrection."[18] I believe that once our reference point has shifted from God to something else, we are worshiping idols. Webber goes on to say this:

> Karl Marx defined a person in terms of work: What do you do? The philosopher Descartes defined a person in terms of mind: What do you think? And the technological revolution defined a person through production: What have you done? Worship that is principally geared toward dispensing intellectual information or pressing for results—massive church memberships or decisions—has already capitulated to the secular attitude. It reduces human personality to a brain or a product, and worship deteriorates into nothing more than information for the mind or a product for the producer.[19]

As Christian referentialists we need to keep referencing all of our art to Christ. We need to keep pointing people to the gospel. Christian worship is declaring through music, sermons, and other art forms that our God is a redemptive God, and he is working in our lives today.

REPRISE

As I think of formalism, expressionism, and referentialism, I am reminded of the privilege of being an artist. One story goes through my mind as I prepare weekly for worship services in the local church. Elvin Jones (drummer with the famous jazz saxophonist, John Coltrane) was interviewed. Elvin was known for playing with an incredible amount of energy. The interviewer asked him, "How do you play with so much energy night after night?" His response was that every time he sat down to play his drums he came to the realization that this could be the last time he would ever play again. He simply played every performance as though it would be his last. It was not long after that interview that the band leader, John Coltrane, passed away.

Remember that we are all in process. To be a great musician is a lifetime endeavor! Learn to enjoy the journey. We have many wonderful opportunities to celebrate Christ. And although we should give our best in every worship service, we will never have a final performance. We will always live to worship the living God.

PART FOUR

BECOMING
A LEADER

INTRODUCTION
TO PART FOUR

AS WORSHIP LEADERS, our fourth objective in becoming a complete worship leader is to develop as leaders. Leadership is not an issue of position or title necessarily. True leadership is primarily an issue of influence. If we are to lead people, we must influence them.

But leadership is more than influence. Leadership, in the Christian context, is also about moving the people of God (through community) to accomplish (through organization) God's purposes (through vision). In order to do this, we must be able to adequately define reality, both with ourselves and with the organization (in this case, the local church). In other words, we must take a hard look at our own lives as well as the current condition of our church and be honest about what needs to change for the purpose of God being glorified.

In the next two chapters, I will speak about demonstration and participation. As leaders, we must demonstrate what we want our followers to do. Then we must get them in on the action. Leadership training is imperative if we are going to worship with others. In the chapter on demonstration, I will be focusing on the personal development of the leader. In the chapter on participation, I will be focusing on leading the people of God in corporate worship. Furthermore, there is a chapter on how to build and lead a worship team. And last, there is a chapter on technology that will conclude this section on leadership.

seven

DEMONSTRATION

THE FIRST STEP to being an influencer is modeling what we want our followers to become. In the area of worship, we must demonstrate what it means to worship the living God. Worship is more than singing songs on Sunday mornings. Worship is about the totality of our lives, about the kind of life we live before the living God. We must reflect a love for Jesus Christ if we are to impact our congregations in the area of worship.

Our people are desperately looking for examples of men and women who really love God. In an age of information, people are looking for role models, not just more ideas on the topic of worship. They need to see a person who loves Jesus if they themselves are to do the same.

Jesus Christ is our ultimate example of what it means to follow after God. Jesus always did what was pleasing to the Father. He never did anything on his own initiative. His was a life of perfect obedience and perpetual worship before the Father. His was a life that modeled a dynamic dependence and relationship with the Father.

Jesus stated in John 13:15, "I have set you an example that you should do as I have done for you." The context of this verse concerns serving one another. This is the passage in which Jesus *demonstrates* service by washing the disciples' feet. Jesus says that he left an example so his disciples would go and do likewise. This in turn would be the Christian ethic: to love even as Jesus loved. We are told in Mark 10:45, "For even the Son of Man did not come to be served, but to serve, and to give his life as a ransom for many."

Jesus did not just teach about service; he demonstrated it by washing the disciples' feet and used that act as an opportunity to teach. So it should be with our leadership; we must first demonstrate what we want people to do.

Much of the time we teach but don't demonstrate. I am the father of four boys. I spend very little time informing my children and lots of time forming them. I primarily do this by example. I first show them what I want them to do. Then I have them model the behavior. I teach them why that particular behavior is so important. Children learn concretely, not abstractly; this is especially true in the early years. I am finding out that adults are the same way; they want an example to follow. Instead of telling them that they *ought* to worship, we need to spend the energy showing them *how* to worship. This requires that we demonstrate through our own behavior what we want them to do.

The apostle Paul takes up this theme when he says in 1 Corinthians 11:1, "Follow my example, as I follow the example of Christ." What a tremendous statement. Can we say the same thing to those whom we lead? Can we say to them, follow my example? Can we first and foremost say that we are following the example of Jesus? If not, we need to make some adjustments and start following Jesus.[1]

DEMONSTRATING WORSHIP IN OUR LIVES

The quote "always preach the gospel and if necessary use words" is attributed to Francis of Assisi. People are watching with anticipation to see what the gospel looks like. This is especially true in an age where image has become the new epistemology. We need to reflect what worship is through demonstrating it in our lives.

This message is especially true for young worship leaders. There are many talented young musicians who can do a wonderful job at leading congregational worship with their voices and with their instruments. But to be a complete worship leader more is required. Paul's message to Timothy should be our standard: "Don't let anyone look down on you because you are young, but set an example for the believers in speech, in life, in love, in faith and in purity" (1 Tim. 4:12).

Be an Example in Speech

According to the apostle Paul, the first area in which we are to be an example is the area of speech. As worship leaders, we need to guard the things that come out of our mouths. Many worship leaders talk too much in the worship service. Sometimes what is said is not wise. Every once in a while what is said is said at the wrong time. We desperately need discretion in the area of our speech.

In the Book of Proverbs we read, "Do you see a man who speaks in haste? There is more hope for a fool than for him" (Prov. 29:20). The first principle in guarding our tongues is to think before we speak. We should pray to know whether what we are about to say is from God.

Proverbs 17:27 states, "A man of knowledge uses words with restraint, and a man of understanding is even-tempered." We learn from this passage that a second way to be an example in speech is by using words concisely and in their right timing. We need to think not only of the thought we want to communicate but of the actual words that will best express that thought.

A third passage that I would like to reference is found in Proverbs 12:18: "Reckless words pierce like a sword, but the tongue of the wise brings healing." Our speech needs to bring healing. This is so important for a worship leader who is trying to lead people in worshiping the God of grace. If our speech is negative, harsh, or abrasive, it cannot be congruent with the praise that flows from our mouth when we are singing or preaching about the love of Christ. We need to make sure that our everyday conversation matches the hymns and songs we sing.

We could look at many passages, but these few communicate the importance of watching our speech as worship leaders. When we lead in worship, we do this both by leading in song *and* by the kind of speech that comes from our mouth. May it be thoughtful, concise, and infused with healing.

Be an Example in Life

Worship leaders need to have kingdom priorities. To do that, we must evaluate our current priorities. Are they in alignment with the Kingdom of God? Do we love what Jesus loves? These are important questions for worship leaders to answer.

Jesus said, "Do not store up for yourselves treasures on earth, where moth and rust destroy, and where thieves break in and steal. But store up for yourselves treasures in heaven, where moth and rust do not destroy, and where thieves do not break in and steal. For where your treasure is, there your heart will be also" (Matt. 6:19–21).

Worship leaders may be tempted to treasure success, recognition, and power. There is nothing more tempting for a worship leader than to be thought of as a great musician and to have a recording contract or have a song published. Jesus said in Matthew 6:33 to "seek first his kingdom and his righteousness, and all these things will be given to you as well." If we set our hearts on the Kingdom of God, God will take care of the rest.

Be an Example in Love

Worship leaders should radiate the love of Christ. Our congregations need to see us passionately in love with God and compassionately in love with people. Our love should be vertical and horizontal. Our desire should be to know Christ intimately and to reach out with kindness, gentleness, and compassion to every person who has been created in the image of God.

Our congregations hear us sing about the love of Christ, but do they see this love reflected in our lives? Do they see that we love the One whom we sing and teach about? Do they see a congruency in our speech and in our example? Do we *demonstrate* a vibrant love with Jesus? This is what makes a worship leader dynamic. If people see our strong desire for God, our times of worship will radiate this kind of message.

Furthermore, our congregations need to know that we love them. People do not care how much you know until they know how much you care. Worship leader, if your congregation knows that you love them, they will more willingly support the leadership you offer to bring about changes you suggest.

I believe that the reason church leaders die on the battlefield of a worship war is because the people think that their pastor does not love them. We try to implement change and our people are not sure whether we care about them. If you demonstrate that you do care about them, you will be able to bring your people along in the area of worship.

Be an Example of Faith

Worship leaders should model faith; we should be examples of both having faith and growing in the faith. Growing in faith is predicated on the assumption that we are rooted in the faith (basic Christian doctrine).

As a worship leader, the one area that has helped me grow in faith has been to study theology. This is why I dedicated the first section of this work to that topic. Suffice it to say, as I have studied my Bible, the reformers, and the Puritans on the basic doctrinal categories, I have grown in faith.

Pisteuo (faith) in its verbal form must have an object. If our faith is in our faith, we will be forever trying to create emotional energy to sustain what we desire to believe in. This is what the Christian Scientist practices.

Our faith is built on nothing less than Jesus Christ and his righteousness; the object of our faith is not our faith but God. We must know our God if we are to have a dynamic faith. The reason I believe that God can heal people in the midst of a worship service is because, for God, nothing is impossible. God will never do anything that contradicts his character. God is gracious, merciful, and compassionate. Healing for God is an issue of arranging molecules. Nothing is too difficult for him. This is the kind of faith that rejuvenates a worship service. When a worship leader has a deep understanding of God, this will be infused into the congregation.

Be an Example of Purity

The last category Paul encourages Timothy to be an example in is purity. Nothing will wreck a worship leader faster than moral compromise. We must know the standard (The Word of God) and the character of God if we are to rightly lead in worship. Our lives must reflect not only a moral purity but a total separation (*qadosh*) as was required of the Levites. We cannot afford to give our people mixed signals of who God is by being a poor example in the area of purity.

If our congregations see that we love Christ and that we have given our lives to him, the songs we sing and the message we preach will have credibility. What gives a messenger credibility is not only the content of what he or she brings to the people but the messenger himself or herself. We must reflect the character of Christ. This is the importance of sanctification. We must continue to grow in holiness. We should demonstrate that the Holy Spirit abides within us. By living for God we demonstrate how to worship God.

If we live chaste, moral lives, people will not be able to say negative things about us. As Paul stated in Titus 2:7–8, "In everything set them an example by doing what is good. In your teaching show integrity, seriousness and soundness of speech that cannot be condemned, so that those who oppose you may be ashamed because they have nothing bad to say about us." This message is for us today. We need to be examples as worship leaders in everything we do. If we live by the Spirit, we "will not gratify the desires of the sinful nature" (Gal. 5:16).

Demonstrating How to Worship

Our congregations need to see that we are people of integrity, demonstrating worship as a lifestyle. But they also need to see that we are willing to express our love to the Savior. Praise is always expressive, active, and demonstrative in the Scriptures. Worship is something we do! It is something that we express.

Psalm 95:1–2, 6, for example, says, "Come let us sing for joy to the Lord, let us shout aloud to the Rock of our salvation. Let us come before him with thanksgiving and extol him with music and song. . . . Come, let us bow down in worship, let us kneel before the Lord our Maker." If we want to implement this psalm with our congregations, we need to be the first to sing, shout, give thanks, extol with music and song, bow down, and kneel before the Lord. If we do this, we are demonstrating what worship looks like according to this psalm. If we want our congregation to lift their hands, we need to demonstrate this. If worship is a part of our lifestyle, people will observe and desire this for themselves.

This is especially important as it pertains to prayer. If you were to teach a new believer how to pray, how would you do it? Would you study a book on prayer together? Would you send the person to a conference on prayer? What would you do?

The most efficient way to teach that young disciple how to pray would be to pray with him or her. Take the person to a prayer meeting where people are praying. That person needs demonstration of what prayer looks like and sounds like in order to learn how to pray. The same is true for having quiet times and learning how to witness.

Great leaders know that people need a demonstration when learning something new. This is true whether they are buying an appliance, learning a skill, or learning how to worship. Teaching about worship is important, but it is not sufficient. We must demonstrate *how* to worship.

How to Respond to God with Passion

When I think of the word *passion*, I think of consumption, devotion, addiction. When you are passionate about something, you cannot get your mind off that object. Your mind is rehearsing how to obtain what you desire. The plans develop. The mind is engaged in analysis for acquisition. You have your emotions escalating in desiring that which you are passionate about. It is just a matter of time before the will is engaged in choosing that which you desire.

The most important dimension of our demonstration of response to God should be that of passion. If we are not passionate about Jesus, we will be passionate about something else. We must guard our hearts. Our passions must be directed toward God. This is the primary work of the Holy Spirit, who is conforming us to the image of Christ. Note these directives from Jesus himself:

> Hearing that Jesus had silenced the Sadducees, the Pharisees got together. One of them, an expert in the law, tested him with this question: "Teacher, which is the greatest commandment in the Law?" Jesus replied: "'Love the Lord your God with all your heart and with all your soul and with all your mind.' This is the first and greatest commandment. And the second is like it: 'Love your neighbor as yourself.' All the Law and the Prophets hang on these two commandments."
>
> MATTHEW 22:34–40

Jesus, quoting from Deuteronomy 6 and Leviticus 19, in essence states that if you will focus on these two commandments, loving God passionately and loving people compassionately, you will keep the Law and the Prophets.

The order is significant. We must first and foremost demonstrate a passion for God. Then and only then will we learn how to love people. Listen to what Joseph Carroll says in his book *How to Worship Jesus Christ*:

> Have you ever noticed in the Pauline epistles that Paul never urges Christians to witness nor has he anything to say about foreign missions? Nothing! How interesting! If you have to constantly be telling people to witness, something is wrong with them. If you always have to be pumping up people to get them interested in foreign missions, something is wrong with the people. What is Paul always doing? He is consistently bringing you to Christ and leaving you with Christ. When Christ is central in the heart of the man, what does the man want to do? He wants to tell others about Jesus, and he will do so effectively. Let

Jesus Christ be central in the heart of a man, and he is going to be burdened and troubled because millions have never heard of Christ. It is going to disturb him and bring him into action. What he needs is not more exhortation; he needs Christ.[2]

A few years ago, I had the opportunity to worship at Jack Hayford's church in Van Nuys, California. When the service began, I felt what I can only describe as the manifest presence of God. I have had this experience during other intimate times of worship. It was not that the music was perfectly done; it was not that the service started and finished right on the hour; it was not even the expositional teaching of Jack Hayford. I believe the difference was that this congregation knew how to show their affection to the Lord Jesus Christ.

The music segment was not merely the warm-up for the sermon. We sang *passionately* to Jesus. It did not matter if it was a hymn or a contemporary praise song. What was important was *whom* we were singing to and how we were executing this privilege. Several different people led in the singing. I think most of them were on the pastoral staff. These were not studio musicians but pastors who had a heart for God leading the body of Christ into worship through their example and encouragement. It was a glorious time of worship.

It is no surprise to me that this congregation is the size that it is. Who would not crave this environment? Church on the Way is truly a centripetal force in the community. People go to that church for one purpose: to meet God. The leaders of this church do not have to create fancy programming to attract visitors and attenders. They have their priorities straight. First, they minister to the Lord. Second, they minister to the body of Christ. Third, they minister to the world. This is how to do church and how to be the church! There is nothing more exciting than to see the people of God expressing their love, with everything that is within them, to the Lord Jesus Christ.

In his book, *Worship His Majesty,* Jack Hayford states that worship is a kingdom activity offered by kingdom people to the King of kings, which brings about a kingdom of God impact on earth. He goes on to say that worship is not only for God but for us. When we worship, the presence of God is manifested. We invite the transcendent realm into the natural realm. God inhabits the praises of his people. Listen to the way Hayford puts it:

> The primary issue is whether we will come and be led before His Throne and seek Him. Because if we do, heaven will break loose on earth! In our church, the passage of nearly two decades has seen tremendous growth in people, an increase in attendance to nearly 10,000 each week, a garnering of nearly 30,000 decisions for Christ during that time span—all flowing from this mind set concerning worship's priority and its purpose.[3]

Why is worship essential to the life of the congregation? It is essential because it breathes life into the church. It is essential because people meet God in an atmosphere of worship. It is essential because it reveals kingdom priority; namely that Jesus is the King of kings, the Lord of lords, and is sovereign over history. In the New Testament, 1 Peter 2:9–10 states, "But you are a chosen people, a royal priesthood, a holy nation, a people belonging to God, that you may declare the praises of him who called you out of darkness into his wonderful light. Once you were not a people, but now you are the people of God; once you had not received mercy, but now you have received mercy." If there is anything that should motivate us to worship Jesus passionately, it should be the fact that God has declared us to be heirs of his kingdom.

When the body of Christ places the worship of Christ in its rightful position, the church will be fulfilling its destiny—providing edification for the body of Christ and demonstrating to the world that there is another, historical story unraveling in addition to our own personal or cultural story. This story is God's story. It is the kingdom of God story. It is the story where Jesus has triumphed over the powers of darkness and death itself. It is the story where God rules. It is the story where Jesus is the King of kings and Lord of lords. It is the story of redemption, of victory, and hope. It is the story where humanity finds fulfillment. It is this story, that if told and expressed regularly, will draw the community into our sanctuaries. This is why worship is vital to the life of the local church.

As we continue to place the worship of Christ in the center of all our activities, the kingdom of God will penetrate the kingdom of darkness. Worship is like a magnet drawing the presence of Christ into the natural realm. As the psalmist said, it is in his presence there is fullness of joy (see Ps. 16:11). May we experience the manifest presence of God as we invite him into our midst through our wholehearted attention and adoration.

The "How-to" of Corporate Worship

Since worship is our response of service based on God's revelation, what exactly should worship look like? It is over this question that many of the "worship wars" exist. The how question concerns form and is also the topic that is covered at many of the worship seminars.

Our worship habits should be in obedience to the Scriptures. Based on the Scriptures, I believe the "how to" question could be answered in three categories: the attitudes of worship, the expressions of worship, and the times of worship.

The Attitudes of Worship

First of all, there are appropriate attitudes that we should have when approaching the Lord. God does not owe us anything. We sometimes approach God as though he existed to serve us. We come to church and demand that he impress us. We move from church to church asking God to entertain us. But worship is not about what we want. Ecclesiastes 5:1 states, "Guard your steps when you go to the house of God. Go near to listen rather than to offer the sacrifice of fools, who do not know that they do wrong." Every week there are people in churches across America who carry around with them the attitude that if the worship service is not prepared just the way they like it, they are not going to participate.

When we approach God we are to have an attitude of humility, reverence, gratefulness, and appreciation for what he has done (see Lev. 10:3; Pss. 29:2; 89:7; 93:5; Hab. 2:20; John 4:24). As worship leaders, we must demonstrate this kind of attitude. The psalmist said, "But I, by your great mercy, will come into your house; in reverence will I bow down toward your holy temple" (Ps. 5:7). Also in Psalm 96:9 it is written, "Worship the LORD in the splendor of his holiness; tremble before him, all the earth."

Therefore, attitude is the starting point for dynamic worship services. We as worship leaders must demonstrate this. When the body of Christ comes together before the throne with humility, all authority will be released on the church to experience the manifest presence of God. When we realize that worship is first and foremost for God, we will relinquish the temptation to design the worship service for us. Attitude is not only the starting place for dynamic worship but the heartbeat behind why we worship.

The Expressions of Worship

The second category the Bible deals with is the variety of physical expressions with which we are to worship God. In his book, *The Hallelujah Factor,* Jack Taylor states that, praise, in its essence, is adoration of God. For a workable definition, however, we must qualify this: praise is always active, assertive, demonstrative, and open. It is not passive, presumptuous, undemonstrative, or secretive. Wherever it is mentioned, movement, action, sounds, and songs are seen and heard.[4]

This is a beautiful definition for praise and for the worship lifestyle. We are to exalt the Lord with everything that is within us. Yet much of the time, we are concerned about what people think. We become intimidated. If we desire for our people to worship void of fear, we must first demonstrate what this looks like. May we learn to express ourselves to the Lord. May we find the freedom to tell the Lord how much we love him.

Our bodies enable us to express what is going on in our souls. The Scriptures speak of uplifted hands, singing voices, playing instruments, bowing down, dancing, and shouting. All of these are activities that we perform with our bodies. Romans 12:1 states, "I urge you therefore, brethren, by the mercies of God, to present your bodies a living and holy sacrifice, acceptable to God, which is your spiritual service of worship" (NASB). Simply put, we are to bless the Lord with everything that is within us. We are to expressively tell him how much we love him, and the only way to do this completely is to engage our bodies in the activity. It is bad theology to say, "You worship that way, but let me worship my way." We do not worship only as far as we feel comfortable in the same way that we do not make ethical decisions as long as they meet our convenience. The world might do this but not people who declare to live by his objective standard of truth.

Historically, God has been known for pushing people out of their comfort zones. If God tells us to sing, then we should sing. If he tells us to lift our hands, then we should lift our hands. If he tells us to prostrate ourselves, then we should prostrate ourselves. God speaks; we respond. Not the other way around. Then and only then will we find the blessing of obedience to God for how we are to praise him. Yes, worship includes the body. And the Scriptures tell us how to appropriate our bodies in worship. The Psalms are a great starting place for more information on how to worship him with everything that is within us. We as worship leaders should be as familiar with the Psalms as we are with the latest choruses.

Now, as to the types of songs we are to sing, we are to sing and speak "psalms, hymns and spiritual songs" (Eph. 5:19). All three of these words mean songs that are prompted by thanksgiving and praise. We have three categories for these types of songs: the Scriptures (as in the Book of Psalms), hymns from church history, and the new songs being written today. Many people tend to go to one extreme or another when it comes to singing the traditional song or the new song. We should do both. Hymns provide theology. "Consider Martin Luther. He called his people 'theological barbarians' and taught basic theology by devoting Thursday evenings to congregational hymn singing. Two centuries later, the Lutheran composer J. S. Bach tells of his congregation singing up to forty stanzas of one hymn."[5] Hymns are transcendent, intellectual, and doctrinal. Buddy Owens, in a worship class I had at Fuller Seminary, said, "the hymns contain memories of the church and a person without memory is mentally ill." I would agree. I would also point out that the hymns keep us singing about the cross and the blood.

On the other hand, we are encouraged to sing the new song; it is in the Scriptures! Psalm 40:3 states that the new song can be a very effective evangelistic tool: "He put a new song in my mouth, a hymn of praise to our God. Many will see and fear and put their trust in the LORD." It has been my experience that churches or movements that have people writing new songs, are the churches and movements that are growing by conversion growth. A case in point would be the Vineyard movement or Christian Assembly with

Tommy Walker. Also, Hillsongs Christian Fellowship in Sydney, Australia, would be an example of this kind of growth.

These churches are not using music only for the purpose of growth; they are using music to worship the Lord. In the process, however, many people are attracted to that environment.

The new songs that are written often provide a balance with traditional hymnody. Choruses tend to be emotional and expressive and emphasize the immanency of the Father. God is both transcendent (different from us—the emphasis of the hymnal) and immanent (he draws near to us as a Father—the emphasis of the choruses). This is not a clean-cut distinction. Many choruses being written today are transcendent modern-day hymns. It is my prayer that members of the body of Christ will learn to love the songs and prayers in the Scriptures, traditional hymnody, and the new songs that God has put in the hearts of the current and upcoming generations.

THE TIMES OF WORSHIP

Concerning the times of worship, the Bible tells us to worship the Lord at all times: "Be joyful always; pray continually; give thanks in all circumstances, for this is God's will for you in Christ Jesus" (1 Thess. 5:16). As Christians, worship should be something that we are constantly engaged in. We should always be thanking the Lord, praying to him, and living lives of obedience.

Yet, we also know that God has asked his people to gather for special occasions. In the Old Testament, God initiated many feasts to commemorate what he had done. Passover would be the pinnacle example.

In the New Testament we read: "On the first day of every week, each one of you should set aside a sum of money in keeping with his income, saving it up, so that when I come no collections will have to be made" (1 Cor. 16:2). We see that Sunday became the new day of worship in Acts 20:7: "On the first day of the week we came together to break bread. Paul spoke to the people and because he intended to leave the next day, kept on talking until midnight." Thus, we see special days are to be observed by Christians. The Lord's Day is a time to worship with the body of Christ.

OBEDIENCE AND WORSHIP

Worship is our response to God as demonstrated in obedient lives and service to him. Allen and Borror state that "the English word worship is wonderfully expressive of the act that it describes. This term comes from the Anglo-Saxon *weorthscipe*, which then was modified to *worthship*, and finally to *worship*. Worship means 'to attribute worth' to something or someone."[6] Our responsive service to God should bring him glory and honor. In the Old Testament, 1 Chronicles 16:28–29 states, "Ascribe to the LORD, O families of nations, ascribe to the LORD glory and strength, ascribe to the LORD the glory due his name. Bring an offering and come before him; worship the LORD in the splendor of his holiness."

Deep in the souls of many Christians is the idea that worship is the music part of the service that precedes the sermon. They talk as if worship only prepares people for the message. Many believe that only forty minutes of uninterrupted, free-flowing worship will get them into the presence of God. Others believe that we need to have the hymns of the faith to get into the presence of God. If a person is living in disobedience, he or she will not be able to come into his presence in forty minutes. We have put more emphasis on the form of worship than on the function of worship. The prophet Amos put it this way:

I hate, I despise your religious feasts; I cannot stand your assemblies. Even though you bring me burnt offerings and

139

grain offerings, I will not accept them. Though you bring choice fellowship offerings, I will have no regard for them. Away with the noise of your songs! I will not listen to the music of your harps. But let justice roll on like a river, righteousness like a never-failing stream!

AMOS 5:21–24

By the time we get to the New Testament, we see that there were very religious people, such as the Pharisees, whose hearts were far removed from God. They focused too much on form and forgot the function of worship. The function of worship, once again, is to bring glory and honor to the Lord by responding to his revelation. It is imperative that we get the function part of worship straight. If we understand that worship is correlated with obedience, we can see that any obedient action will bring glory and honor to the Lord. Therefore, if the Lord tells me to forgive even as I have been forgiven, by being obedient to that word, I am bringing worship to the Lord. If I have something against my brother or sister and I refuse to get things right with that person before coming and offering my sacrifice to the Lord, God will not accept my offering. He has clearly stated his will concerning this issue in Matthew 5:23–24. If the Lord tells me to incorporate lifting my hands, shouting, singing, yea even dancing, then by doing this I will bring glory and honor to him.

Prayer and Worship

Another area that is closely associated to obedience and service to God is the role of prayer in our Christian lives. When we pray, we are basically communicating that we want God's will to be accomplished. Prayer, etymologically, remains an issue of appealing to the Father. Although prayer happens in the context of a relationship with God, it is not the relationship in and of itself. Rather, the essence of prayer is the imploring that takes place on the part of the needy to the One who supplies all of our needs in Christ Jesus (Phil. 4:19). F. B. Meyer said "the greatest tragedy is not unanswered prayer but unoffered prayer." Jesus said, "Until now, you have asked for nothing in My name; ask, and you will receive, that your joy may be made full" (John 16:24 NASB).

In his chapter entitled "Epicletic Doxology" from the book *Themes and Variations for a Christian Doxology*, Hughes Oliphant Old states, "the word epiclesis means 'to call upon, to make an appeal to someone or address oneself to someone.' When the faithful call upon God in times of need, God is glorified. The very act of calling upon God's name is itself worship." Old continues by saying, "The god of the philosophers may not want to hear of the troubles of the world, but it is not the god of the philosophers whom we worship."[7] When we cry out to God, we are communicating that only he is able to meet all of our needs. The result is worship, in that it is our heartfelt response to the revelation that apart from him, we can do nothing!

The Psalms are the best resource to train ourselves on how to cry out to God in prayer and worship. It is there that we meet people like David, who struggled with fears just like us: "O LORD, how my adversaries have increased! Many are rising up against me. Many are saying of my soul, 'There is no deliverance for him in God'" (NASB). But it is in the context of his relationship with God that he can finally say, "But thou, O LORD, art a shield about me, My glory, and the One who lifts my head" (Ps. 3:1–3 NASB). In the midst of our fears, do we cast all our anxiety upon him knowing that he cares for us (1 Peter 5:7)? When we do, we are at the very heart of the matter, worshiping God.

Sacrifice and Worship

Not only is worship described as our response to God, it is the specific type of response we render, namely that of sacrifice. "I urge you therefore, brethren, by the mercies of God, to present your bodies a living and holy sacrifice, acceptable to God which is your spiritual service of worship" (Rom. 12:1 NASB). I find it intriguing that week after week we go to a "worship service" yet never make the correlation between these two terms in our daily lives. To worship God is to serve God. To worship God is to give our lives to him. It is the worship leader that must demonstrate this ministry of service and sacrifice.

Again David Peterson offers some insightful information on this subject when he states: "A common factor in the three terms describing Israel's vocation here ('my treasured possession,' 'a kingdom of priests,' 'a holy nation') is the note of separation from the nations in order to be uniquely at God's disposal. The Israelites were drawn into a special or sanctified relationship with God from amongst the nations. . . . Just as a priest is separated from an ancient society in order to serve it and serves it by his distinctiveness, so Israel serves her world by maintaining her distance and her difference from it."[8] We will be engaging in worship when we decide to give our lives to God as a living and holy sacrifice.

As I speak of this idea of sacrificing to God, I once again go back to the premise that this is how we respond to God. God initiates worship; we respond to him. We must see the importance of the idea that worship requires us to bring something. Ralph Martin states:

> The distinctive genius of corporate worship is the two-beat rhythm of revelation and response. God speaks; we answer. God acts; we accept and give. God gives; we receive. As a corollary to this picture, worship implies a code word for man's offering to God: *sacrifice*. The worshiper is not a passive, motionless recipient, but an active participant, called upon to "make an offering."[9]

Reprise

   As worship leaders, we must demonstrate the intricacies of worship such as a generous spirit, a worshipful attitude, a person who worships God with body as well as with heart, and a life totally lived for Christ. If parishioners see this modeled, they will be more inclined to participate in this worship lifestyle. Participation will be the topic of the next chapter for this is an important goal for the worship leader: how to get the body of Christ engaged in worship.

eight

PARTICIPATION

WHEN WE GATHER every Sunday, a goal of congregational worship should be participation. Such involvement is a biblical mandate, and every worship leader should take it seriously. The complete worship leader is ultimately completed by the body of Christ.

In worship, the people for whom Christ has died are responding to God. When we gather at the table, we do this together. When we sing hymns, we do it collectively. When we study and read the Word of God, we study as a family.

There is nothing more discouraging to see than the body of Christ in disunity. There is still a greater tragedy, and that is when believers are in disagreement concerning the worship service, for a church that does not worship together is ultimately a disruption to the Kingdom of God.

The body of Christ is never more unified than when it is praying together, singing together, exhorting each other, studying together, and partaking of the sacraments together. A worship leader, through prayer and planning, must make sure that the church to which he or she has been called is worshiping in unity week after week.

Worship is not a spectator sport. One of my concerns today is the entertainment model of "worship." The idea is that people show up and get entertained by a praise band or choir. Then the pastor steps up to the microphone and takes over. Not once during such a service are the people encouraged to be part of the action. We must remember that worship is something that *we*, the people of God, perform. "Worship is an active response to God whereby we declare His worth. Worship is not passive, but is participative. Worship is not simply a mood; it is a response. Worship is not just a feeling; it is a declaration."[1] Therefore, it is we, God's chosen people, who must declare his praises. We must engage in obedience when it comes to praising God.

EVERYONE HAS SOMETHING TO CONTRIBUTE

When I speak of believers worshiping together, this is not some idealism I have but rather a clear biblical command. The apostle Paul gives us instructions on how we are to function as the body of Christ:

> For the grace given me I say to every one of you: Do not think of yourself more highly than you ought, but rather think of yourself with sober judgment, in accordance with the measure of faith God has given you. Just as each of us has one body with many members, and these members do not all have the same function, so in Christ we who are many form one body, and each member belongs to all the others. We have different gifts, according to the grace given us. If a man's gift is prophesying, let him use it in proportion to his faith. If it is serving, let him serve; if it is teaching, let him teach; if it is encouraging, let him encourage; if it is contributing to the needs of others, let him give generously; if it is leadership, let him govern diligently; if it is showing mercy, let him do it cheerfully.

ROMANS 12:3–8

Paul's comment to the church at Rome is equally true for us: We are not to think of ourselves more highly than we ought. In the context of this passage, Paul is saying that part of offering our bodies is allowing all members of the body to contribute. Pride and one-upmanship will kill the congregational spirit of worship.

Paul states that we are one with many different functions. We all have different gifts, according to the grace given to us. We must encourage and *permit* the use of each other's gifts as God designed. If we do not permit all members to use their gifts, we quench the working of the Spirit of God. Therefore, we need to make the necessary adjustments for the body of Christ to function according to its gifting.

> The body is a unit, though it is made up of many parts; and though all its parts are many, they form one body. So it is with Christ. For we were all baptized by one Spirit into one body—whether Jews or Greeks, slave or free—and we were all given the one spirit to drink. Now the body is not made up of one part but of many. If the foot should say, "Because I am not a hand, I do not belong to the body," it would not for that reason cease to be part of the body. And if the ear should say, "Because I am not an eye, I do not belong to the body," it would not for that reason cease to be part of the body. If the whole body were an eye, where would the sense of hearing be? If the whole body were an ear, where would the sense of smell be? But in fact God has arranged the parts in the body, every one of them, just as he wanted them to be. If they were all one part, where would the body be? As it is, there are many parts, but one body. The eye cannot say to the hand, "I don't need you!" And the head cannot say to the feet, "I don't need you!" On the contrary, those parts of the body that seem to be weaker are indispensable, and the parts that we think are less honorable we treat with special honor. And the parts that are unpresentable are treated with special modesty, while our presentable parts need no special treatment. But God has combined the members of the body and has given greater honor to the parts

that lacked it, so that there should be no division in the body, but that its parts should have equal concern for each other. If one part suffers, every part suffers with it; if one part is honored, every part rejoices with it.

1 CORINTHIANS 12:12–26

Again, Paul stated to the church at Corinth that they needed to see their interdependence upon one another. The most "insignificant" member of the body of Christ is the most "significant." The rest of the body cannot function without its contribution.

It is God who has arranged the parts in the body. It is God who has gifted the members of the body. God has appointed apostles, prophets, and teachers. Not all of us have the same gifts. But all of us do have the same obligation to *use* our gifts in conjunction with the rest of the body of Christ.

The key thought is that everyone should have something to contribute when they come to worship. *How far we have drifted from the Scriptures.* Instead we have celebrities in the pulpits, superstars leading singing, and professionals doing the visual arts while the people of God function as non-contributors in the worship service. What a show we can put on! Yet, the church is not a circus where people show up to see the professionals perform. The church is a place where the saints come and participate in the worship service.[2] In America, worship has been taken captive by the trends of the times.

THE TREND OF CONSUMERISM

Consumerism, as in the promotion of the consumer's interest, has plagued our churches. We consume religion. It begins with the preaching. People want to attend a church where the preacher hits a home run every Sunday. It is not coincidental that growing churches in America have a dynamic pulpit ministry. I am not discouraging a strong pulpit ministry. We should have dynamic preaching in all of our churches. What I am challenging is the attitude of the people who sit in the pews. If the preaching is off on a particular day, they might not come back. People want service or more appropriately as Rick Warren would say "serve-us."

Another way people demand service is in the area of music. People judge the quality of their church by the music program. If organs and choirs are not present, they cannot worship. If there is not a forty-minute segment of uninterrupted music with a praise band, they cannot worship. This is nonsense! This is American consumerism.

In 1985, I was in Romania with the Continental Singers. Our mission was to encourage the body of Christ in the then Communist country. Many of our services were unauthorized (underground). The routine was we would receive a knock from our leadership on the door of our youth hostel. We would get in a van (led by one of the nationals hosting us), drive down a block, take a right, down an alley, get off, walk a quarter of a mile with the intention of losing the government officials who were following us, and then show up in a building with hundreds of Romanian worshipers.

The picture is still clear in my mind. Here were youth, children, the elderly, working families, all in unison, with different instruments (mandolins, guitars, flügelhorns, and violins), singing praise to God and worshiping the Lord with a loud voice. Some of the hymns were recognizable. The song I remember them singing in Romanian was "Leaning on the Everlasting Arms." It was infused with meaning and purpose as they faced the persecution of an awful dictator.

What impressed me more than anything else was the involvement of these believers. They were all doing something. Not one person was there consuming but rather participating wholeheartedly. This is what we so desperately lack in American churches.

THE TREND OF SPECTATORSHIP

The trend of spectatorship is comparative to consumerism. In essence, the difference is that consumerism is driven by utilitarianism and spectatorship is driven by entertainment. Not only do we want the best deal, we want to be entertained.

Spectatorship is also driven by a nation that worships sports and sporting events. We enjoy nothing more than going to a football game and watching our favorite teams compete for a championship. We love to watch the Super Bowl, the World Series, the Stanley Cup, and the NBA playoffs. Yet the local church is not the place to be a spectator. The church is not a stadium or a stage; it is a living organism organized to mobilize the body of Christ into action.

It has been said that the church in many ways *does* represent sports. You have overworked pastors on the playing field with underworked parishioners in the bleachers doing the cheerleading. The church should be more like an army of soldiers preparing for war than a Broadway stage production. We are all to play our part in order to be salt and light.

To become complete worship leaders, we need to mobilize all the participants in our worship services. But how do we get them to participate?

GETTING PEOPLE TO PARTICIPATE

Advertise

Participation begins before people arrive at your church. On your answering machines, do you give clear information over the phone? Do you have clear information in the phone book as to when your services begin? I cannot tell you how many times we have received worshipers into our sanctuary because they had read our ad in the phone book. Do not underestimate the importance of using the yellow pages. Do your marquees give clear, concise information? I have seen marquees used for cute sayings instead of providing facts on worship times for the community. Visitors need to know when to attend the worship services. Reading unnecessary info is like reaching an answering machine with a lengthy greeting and having to wait several seconds to leave a message. Whenever you waste people's time, you will lose the potential of attracting worshipers.

Do you have signage on your property that tells how to get to the sanctuary? Do people know when the worship service starts? And think about how radio, TV, and newspaper announcements and a web site could advertise your church. These overlooked details fail to take into consideration a spirit of hospitality when trying to attract worshipers to your sanctuary.

Greeters and Ushers

Your warmest, most gregarious people should greet guests in your foyer. Whether you realize it or not, what happens in the initial contact can determine whether or not people will participate in the worship service.

In the hotel business, most of the training goes into the front desk people. If guests encounter warm, friendly people when they arrive, they are likely to return. So it is with churches. Visitors need to meet people that are hospitable.[3] This will empower them to worship in the service. We cannot underestimate the importance of warm, friendly greeters and ushers.

Ushers must be ready to respond to questions asked by visitors. If a young mother comes in and inquires about the nursery, that usher must communicate where the nursery is located.

The usher must also work to create better participation by seating people close together and close to the platform. It is my observation that people sing out and participate more if they are together in proximity.

Ushers should offer a bulletin that will aid the worshiper. If the bulletin is used as a Sunday morning newspaper, this can be a distraction to participation in worship. Get the clutter out of your worship bulletin if you desire to use it to prompt worship. This, of course, is not the responsibility of the usher but of the worship leader. A solution for where to have the weekly announcements is to place them in an information center where people can pick them up.[4] You could also put the information on PowerPoint before and after the service.

The Senior Pastor's Role

The next area, if the congregation is to participate in the worship service, is the warmth of the senior pastor. Whether the pastor offers opening remarks, a formal call to worship, or a formal welcome, the people will be put at ease and therefore more likely to participate in worship. The senior pastor can also establish what is accepted etiquette in your church. For example, Jack Hayford at Church on the Way will frequently communicate to the people that it is biblical to raise hands in surrender or praise to the Lord. He will gently instruct the people what is acceptable praise to the Lord. This communicates that the senior pastor is excited about congregational worship.

Model Participation from the Platform

The worship leader must model participation from the platform. You have a choice to follow the direction of Psalm 150 (to praise the Lord with as many instruments as possible) or to put on a performance by yourself. In some churches, only studio musicians are on the platform. Balance is needed here. Though you do not want an amateur band leading worship, you should find a place for everyone to participate. I believe the parable of the talents has great application here (Matt. 25:14–30). Some will have five talents vocally; some will only have one talent. In other words, people may be at different stages of musical ability. Recognize and accommodate the variety of musical abilities in your church. Some of your singers might be studio musicians, and some may not even be able to read music. All who have a heart for the Lord should be encouraged to participate.

One way that I have dealt with this is to create ensembles that give proper placement for the talent of the individual. In my choir, everyone is allowed to sing. In the praise team, only those with more specialized voices (singing in the contemporary idiom, flexibility with styles, good intonation, and ability to execute syncopated rhythms) may sing. Not every singer can sing in this ensemble. Everyone can participate at some level, however.

Another example of how to get everyone to participate is to do an informal audition. I recently had one of our junior highers approach me about playing the drums. When I auditioned him (I asked him to play different styles: a jazz swing, a Latin beat, a rock beat, and a slow song) he needed growth in the areas of coordination and rhythm (the most important element for a percussionist). I could not have him play the drums at that time. I did tell him that he could play other percussion instruments such as the cabasa and the tambourine, and I encouraged him to take private lessons. He took me up on my offer and in time will probably be our primary drummer. Everyone has a place to participate on the platform. Recovery of "life together" in Christ, to use Bonhoeffer's phrase, would go a long way to set our worship as a corporate exercise and deliver modern congregations from "ministerial monopoly" with one person conducting a virtuoso performance.[5]

Whenever people come into our church, they are surprised to see many people on the platform leading in worship. I must emphasize that we are not a mega church. Rather, we are a church with a high participation factor. We try to provide a place for everyone to be involved.

The other ways in which you can model participation from the platform are clapping, lifting hands, and other physical expressions of worship. You too are communicating what is acceptable worship etiquette in your church by what you do or do not do on the platform. If the people see you lift your hands, they will be more inclined to do this themselves. If members of the congregation see the members of the praise team expressing their love to the Lord, they will do this themselves. The congregation will take their cue from the front concerning acceptable expressions of worship.

Give Clear Instruction

If you want your people to participate, tell them what to do. If you are singing hymns, tell them which stanzas you want them to sing. If you are singing choruses, let them know if you want them to sing on the verses or just on the chorus.

There are many ways of doing this without breaking the flow in the transitional material. List your intentions in the bulletin and let the congregation know the instructions are there. If you are using an overhead projector, slides, or PowerPoint, let the congregation know by projecting the words onto the screen.

If you are in a context where the people intuitively know what to do, praise God that you have a church where people just make it happen. On the other hand, if you are in a church like mine, not only do the people want to know what to do, the visitor is also appreciative of the effort to include him or her. Never assume that people instinctively know what to do.

Choose Songs That Are Singable

I have found the wisdom of Jack Hayford extremely helpful when it comes to the balance of using new and old
music. One important element when introducing a new
song is providing something that is familiar. Listen to what
Hayford says:

> Don't overwhelm people with the new. We usually begin
> the service with something familiar, perhaps with a hymn
> like "All Hail the Power of Jesus' Name" or "Holy, Holy,
> Holy." And whenever we stretch people to experience a
> new dimension of worship, we immediately come back to
> something they're familiar with. So after leading people in
> a new song where I've had them join hands, I will ask them
> to release their hands and sing some old standard. People
> enjoy new expressions of worship more if the service con-
> tains elements they already are comfortable with. . . .
> Another boundary I call the "quantity quotient." People
> can take only so much newness. Too much is an overload.
> We must operate in their comfort zone, even as we push
> the border of that zone further and further out.[6]

In all honesty, I struggle with this. I love to keep learning, growing, and expanding. I love to keep trying new and
fresh material. It is the innovator in me. Yet the people I
lead cannot handle constant change. If we are never changing anything, we will stagnate. On the other hand, if we
are changing too much too quickly, we will introduce panic.
The balance is progressive change. By nature, we are all
creatures of habit. That is not necessarily good or bad; it's
the way it is. We can find the balance by introducing the
new while retaining the familiar.

Choose songs that are singable for the congregation. I
have found that a good range is middle C below the treble
staff up to D in the staff. The key of the song does not matter; it is the melody line that matters. If you are pushing

your congregation to be constantly singing an E or higher, it will be strenuous for them. If you have too many notes below middle C, this too will be uncomfortable. Remember, our goal is to have people singing.

If you are introducing songs with overly syncopated rhythms, you may frustrate your congregation. This has a lot to do with the ethnicity of your congregation. If you are leading worship in a Puerto Rican community where the music (Salsa) is syncopated, you will not have difficulty. If you are leading worship in an African American community, you will not have difficulty. It is my experience that Hispanic and African American music is normally syncopated.

In many congregations, it will be difficult to pull off syncopated rhythms if the people are used to singing from hymnals; in hymnals, melodic lines generally enter and end on the beat, not on the offbeat. Please do not interpret that I am saying that you can never do syncopated music. I am saying that many worship leaders need wisdom when it comes to song selection.[7]

You must also consider the melodic line when introducing a song. If you have a singable melodic line and fairly easy non-syncopated rhythms, you will have a better chance of hitting this mark. If you want *everyone* to participate, you need to think about everyone when you select music. You need to think of nonmusical people trying to learn the songs you are introducing.

The reason musicals such as the *Sound of Music* and *Oklahoma* have been so popular over the years is because of the melodies that remain with you long after the musical is over. So it should be when choosing congregational worship songs. Choose or compose songs with memorable melodies. Not only must our songs be theologically grounded, they must have a great melody line. If you choose a song and the people tell you the next week that they have not been able to get that song out of their mind, you have chosen a winner.

To find a song that works rhythmically, look at the break-down syllabically. Song is poetry put to music. We know that both words and rhythm are important in poetry; so it should be with song. Words should mean something. We must also arrange these words in such a way that there is rhythm. This will make a melody more singable and in turn empower the congregation to participate.

Create a Worship Flow

The next way to get your people to participate is to create a service that has some sense of congruity. Many worship services in Protestant churches are too fractured and interrupted. The attention of the people is turned from God to the upcoming event for the week. All the elements—announcements, offerings, singing, preaching, testimonies—need to tie together.

An ideal way of putting a service together is thematically. After the senior pastor outlines a sermon schedule, the music director can put together music, drama, testimony, and Scripture readings that will complement the sermon. The thematic approach is a very powerful way of acquiring momentum. I would also think of the emotional flow of the worship service. People get bored if everything is always at the same energy level.

Putting the service together musically helps the flow. Do not go back and forth from fast to slow songs. Keep the fast songs together, the medium tempo songs together, and the slow songs together. But when energy begins to drop, make the shift. Keep two or three songs in the same key and then modulate up a half step or a step on the last song to create a sense of finality. Know the key, the meter, and the text of the worship songs. Also be aware of the song getting too high for the congregation to sing. Learn how to modulate appro-priately and how to work with open chord progressions for prayer times or spontaneous singing. For the most part, interruption of flow is due to the lack of planning and training.[8]

Instill a Desire to Know God

Ultimately, participation in worship is an issue of the heart. If you really desire to see your people participate in the worship service, you need to pray that they would be filled with the Spirit of God to overflowing. They must be committed to Jesus Christ if they are going to offer their songs to him.

For people to engage in the worship lifestyle, they must have a heart for Jesus. All the gimmicks you try to pull off in the worship service will degenerate into mere manipulation. What your church needs is not just some prompting but a passion for the Lord Jesus Christ. One of the things that I admire within many of the renewal movements is that many people genuinely do have a longing for the Lord. They come to these churches because they want to know more of the goodness of God and the reality of being filled with his Spirit. Allen and Borror put it so well:

> The lesson which seems to require constant rediscovery is the fact that worship is not primarily a state of the art but rather a state of heart. By state of heart we mean the driving desire behind the worship life of the believer. In both Testaments the Scripture is clear regarding the statement of a heart condition. *These words, which I am commanding you today, shall be on your heart* (Deut. 6:6 NASB).

God is the strength of my heart and my portion forever.

(PS. 73:26 NASB)

Watch over your heart with all diligence, for from it flow the springs of life.

(PROV. 4:23 NASB)

With the heart man believes, resulting in righteousness.

(ROM. 10:10 NASB)

Let us draw near with a sincere heart in full assurance of faith.

(HEB. 10:22; AN EXCELLENT BIBLICAL DEFINITION
OF WORSHIP. NASB)

When the heart is set upon God, true worship will not depend upon outward stimulus, it will be in constant progress. Exhortations like "Pray without ceasing," and "Seek the Lord and His strength, seek His face continually," or "All you do in word and deed, do to the glory of God," will take on their intended meaning. This means that all of life becomes a worship service. If Christians were devotedly practicing this lifestyle, a corporate service could not miss being a great blessing, for it would simply be a continuation of a worship service begun days (or weeks or months) before.[9]

As a worship leader, I am always praying that our people will have a heart for Christ. I am continually asking that the Father would give us, as a local congregation, a desire to know him more. Those within my congregation know this because I have a tendency to do the same thing in the service itself. Every time I begin to pray in the worship service, I find myself praying the first two verses of Psalm 42: "As the deer pants for streams of water, so my soul pants for you, O God. My soul thirsts for God, for the living God. When can I go and meet with God?" Oh that the Lord God would give us a desire for him alone. Oh that we would worship daily at his feet.

When I think of this aspect of worshiping God with our hearts, I am reminded of the Samaritan woman. In the midst of this conversation about living water, the Samaritan woman asks about the "where" of worship. The conversation of the Samaritan woman and Jesus in the fourth chapter of John comes into focus. The Samaritans were used to worshiping on Mount Gerizim and the Jews in Jerusalem. Jesus answered the woman's question by saying that "a time is coming when you will worship the Father neither on this mountain nor in Jerusalem." Jesus then goes on to say that "true worshipers will worship the Father in spirit and truth, for they are the kind of worshipers the Father seeks. God is spirit, and his worshipers must worship in spirit and in truth."

In response to the question of the Samaritan woman, Jesus implied that worship was not an issue of being at the right location but rather in a right relationship. If you do not have a relationship with the Father, you can go to Jerusalem and still not meet God. On the other hand, if you have that relationship with God, you can worship on Mount Gerizim, Jerusalem, or in New York City. In essence, worship is dependent on your relationship with God. Therefore, worship is more about a lifestyle. Chuck Kraft tells a wonderful little story to emphasize this point.

> Two men were asked to read a passage of Scripture in public. One of them was a great orator, the other a rural pastor. The one read it with oratorical brilliance, the other with feeling and passion. Why, it was asked, did the pastor's reading move the audience more than that of the orator? Because, came the reply, though the orator knew the passage he read and had a formal relationship with God, the pastor knew the Author of the passage in quite a different way.[10]

REPRISE

When I think of the question of where we are to worship, I cannot help but think of Psalm 133: "How good and pleasant it is for brethren to dwell together in unity . . . for there the LORD commanded the blessing, even life for evermore" (KJV). When the body of Christ comes together in unity to worship the Father, there is tremendous blessing in the midst of that congregation.

Therefore, the where question could be partly answered by stating that worship should happen at the church and with the church. We are blessed to be able to congregate every Lord's Day to worship Christ with other Christians. What a tremendous privilege it is for us to come together like this.

nine

BUILDING AND LEADING A WORSHIP TEAM

THIS CHAPTER IS a biographical sketch of what the Lord has allowed me to accomplish at my own church. There are no easy answers when it comes to putting together a group of dedicated musicians. But, may these ideas contribute to a dynamic worship ministry in your own context.

PRAYER—DEPENDENCE ON THE LORD

The Lord has been instructing me how to depend upon him through prayer; he has allowed me to fail again and again whenever I plan and strategize without first seeking his guidance (Prov. 3:5–6). Before I do anything, I must pray.

John 16:24 states, "Until now, you have asked for nothing in My name; ask, and you will receive, that your joy may be made full" (NASB). Jesus says that we do not have because we do not ask. This statement is repeated again and again in his teachings. Matthew 7:7–8 says, "Ask, and it shall be given to you; seek, and you shall find; knock, and it shall be opened to you. For every one who asks receives, and he who seeks finds, and to him who knocks it shall be opened" (NASB).

Five years ago, I began to practice what these verses were telling me to do. For example, I had been desperately wanting a drummer. Every time I put an ad in the bulletin, I got no response. I asked people if they knew family members or friends who played the drums. Nobody knew a drummer.

Then I began to ask the Lord to give us a drummer. I asked the musicians to pray that God would give us a drummer. We prayed before and after rehearsals. We also began to thank the Lord that he would eventually give us a drummer for we knew that it was the will of God that he be praised with loud and resounding cymbals (Ps. 150:5; 1 John 5:14–15).

Four months after we began to pray this way, our first drummer showed up. Not only did God send us a drummer, he sent us a very skilled musician. God gave in response to prayer.

Every fall quarter, God shows me this lesson again when I am recruiting for a choir. When I get on the phone and begin to ask people to join the choir, I will get the typical response: "I am too busy to be involved in a choir this quarter." Then I start to become anxious and worried that I am not going to have a choir. God reminds me of his Word: "Be anxious for nothing, but in everything by prayer and supplication with thanksgiving let your requests be made known to God. And the peace of God, which surpasses all comprehension, shall guard your hearts and your minds in Christ Jesus" (Phil. 4:6–7 NASB).

For us to build and lead a worship team, prayer must be a priority. We must ask God to supply people who have a heart for him. We must pray for wisdom to choose the right songs for the upcoming Sunday. We need to be in prayer at all times.

MUSICIANS ATTRACT MUSICIANS

The next principle to keep in mind when building and leading a worship team is that musicians attract musicians. We attract not who we want but who we are. In other words, you can define a worship team all you want, but until you actually put someone up front, you will never begin the process of attracting musicians.

If you want to attract more choir members, you need to get your choir out of the practice room and onto the platform. People will not join a choir if they do not know that one exists. At Bethany, we currently have the following lead in worship on a regular basis: the praise band, the orchestra, the adult choir, the children's choir, the pianist, the organist, and the dance team.

Again, to emphasize how musicians attract musicians, I would like to share with you how a chamber orchestra developed at Bethany Church. Four years ago, I decided to put a brass quintet together for Christmas. I was a trumpet major in college and thought it would be a lot of fun to use this kind of ensemble for preludes, offertories, and postludes during this festive season. That year we had two trumpets, a trombone, a French horn, and a baritone—the perfect brass quintet. We had a wonderful time leading in worship and praising the Lord.

When January arrived, I had people coming to me and telling me they played the clarinet, the flute, the violin, the bassoon, and so forth. They asked if they could play with the brass quintet. My answer was an immediate yes. We had people at all levels of ability pulling out their instruments. What started as a brass quintet ended up as a small chamber orchestra.

Open and Closed Policies

When I started at Bethany, I decided I wanted to build a community of worshipers. As the Lord brought musicians at different levels musically, I had to try to figure out where to place people. I do not always hold formal auditions for every ensemble, yet I have ways of determining where people are musically. Use auditions when necessary and for the purpose of expanding your music ministry, not restricting complete participation.

If I need a soloist for a choir anthem, I spontaneously ask individuals who I think can sing the solo to sing it during the rehearsal. I look for a particular quality of voice to suit the anthem, and I want to hear what it sounds like with the choir. After I have listened to a few individuals, I will ask if there are others who would like to try the solo. If I am not satisfied, or if response is low, I will then hold an audition to choose the right voice.

I never have the best soloist sing all of the solos. Rather, I try to get as many people involved as possible. If an individual needs extra practice I work with him or her until the piece sounds the way I envision it being performed.

I allow anyone to sing in the choir. Again, I do not consistently hold formal auditions as those can be very intimidating. Yet I will hold an audition if a person is not certain which part to sing and says something like, "I do not know whether I should be a tenor or bass."

Although I do not hold formal auditions, I do ask people to have the following qualities if they want to be a part of the choir: First of all, I ask them to have a heart for God. I want to make sure that they are committed to having quiet times and are longing to know the Lord more intimately. The reasoning for this is simple: We lead out of who we are. We are the message, not just the words we sing. Second, I ask them to be teachable and be flexible.

Sometimes I will have choir members try certain musical exercises, and they need to be flexible enough to not think these are silly. Last of all, I ask them to have the courtesy to let me know, ahead of time, their vacation schedules and when they are going to miss rehearsals. I usually return the favor by having a performance schedule printed for the whole quarter at the beginning of the choir season. Then they know what they are committing to for that quarter.

The choir is a place where one can enter at any musical level. Having this kind of open policy also requires some wisdom concerning the selection of music. I am concerned that our people at Bethany have a worshipful experience, and if a simple yet musical piece can accomplish that, then I am satisfied. But I always try to provide a challenge for the choir as well.

I also have an open policy for the orchestra in which we have people at different levels playing their instruments. Again, my only reason for holding an audition for this ensemble would be to determine *what* the musician can play, not *if* he or she will play. I will not allow people to play on every song or in every section of a piece if they are having difficulty with that piece.

For example, I have had a junior high student play the clarinet in the orchestra while sitting next to a more advanced clarinet player. The beginner was encouraged to play the passages he could and to sit out the passages he could not play. The more advanced clarinet player became a mentor to the younger player.

This also happened in the trombone section. We need to give every person a place to play. We need to give every willing vocalist a place to sing. Yet we both know that if that person is a beginner, we will not give them a solo. We need to have a place for everyone but not every place for everyone.

For the more advanced musicians, I have special ensembles. For instance, I do not have an open policy in the praise band; I hand select the musicians for this group. The same is true for the seasonal a cappella ensemble that I have for Christmas. Just as you need to allow younger musicians an entrance point, you need a special place for more advanced musicians.

If you are going to build and lead a worship team, you need to get people involved. You will need to be patient and wise. You will need to know where to place people and how to effectively communicate your desire for both inclusion and exclusion.

PROVIDE A CHALLENGE

At Bethany I constantly try to provide a challenge for our music groups. If I give music to the choir that they do not need to practice, rehearsals will be boring. The same is true for the orchestra or praise team. There is nothing more rewarding than to work on a piece of music and experience the moment when it all comes together. This builds hope, faith, and accomplishment.

Occasionally I have gone too far in my expectations and have discouraged people by giving them a piece of music that they simply could not perform. This contributes to frustration. It is best to avoid this.

BUILD COMMUNITY

Another way of building and leading a worship team is to build community. I have done this simply by breaking up into small groups at the end of rehearsals and having each group pray for the various needs that are present. It is amazing how powerful this can be for building community. I have discovered that these prayer times might be the only opportunity during the week that members of the group have to pray with someone.

Social times are another way of building community. Have some fun by scheduling a potluck or an end-of-the-quarter party and celebrate what the Lord has done in your worship services over the quarter. Something my wife and I have done in trying to build community is going out for lunch with different people in the worship community after the Sunday services.

The ultimate way to build community is to have a retreat. I have had the privilege of leading worship for the Navigators' Colorado Retreats. This has been a wonderful time to take my praise band up to the mountains for a weekend and lead in worship and hear great speakers.

BE OPEN TO NEW IDEAS

This last year we started a dance ministry at Bethany. One of our choir members asked me if she could show me a dance she choreographed for the Good Friday service. I was eager to see what she put together. It turned out to be very worshipful. Because of the positive response we received, I asked if she could pull a dance team together as a regular part of our worship services. My next goal is to incorporate poetry reading as well as more visual art. We have people within our congregation whose art needs to be exposed.

The people you lead have many wonderful ideas. Find ways to solicit feedback; have brainstorming sessions where you collaborate ideas. I rely on the people in each ensemble to give me new ideas on a regular basis. I tell them to listen for new songs on the radio that we might be able to use in our worship services. I also ask them to bring back ideas when they visit a church during a vacation or business trip. Get your people making decisions with you and you will help them feel as if they are contributing to the formation of your worship ministry.

PROVIDE SKILL AND LEADERSHIP TRAINING

I have had local artists come in and offer workshops for our worship participants. For example, last year I had Bob Hoose, writer and producer of The Jeremiah People, come in and do a drama workshop. This was a wonderful opportunity to discuss the visual aspect of what we are doing on the platform.

I have also taken some of my key leaders to leadership conferences such as *Communicating to Change Lives* with John Maxwell and Bill Hybels. This is a good launching pad for a discussion about the need to use leadership gifts. I am currently in a leadership development phase at Bethany and am realizing that if we are to grow, I need qualified people to help me lead the various ensembles.

Skill and leadership training is a must, whether it is studying a book together, going to conferences, hosting workshops, or taking time out in rehearsals to teach. This kind of training will allow you to continue to grow as a worship community.

DEFINE ROLES AND EXPECTATIONS

When putting a worship team together, telling people what role you want them to play is helpful. In my praise band I will instruct the drum, bass, and guitar players to focus on rhythm and the pianist to focus on harmony; I will then provide additional choral harmony on the keyboard. Next I will tell the horn section to provide the necessary "fills" for the spaces at the end of a phrase. In working with the choir, I have the members sing softer when they are in unison and louder when the music goes into parts. Exceptions are only when the musical score dictates otherwise.

Nothing will frustrate musicians more than a director who does not know what he or she wants to accomplish. Musicians are used to having mentors, teachers, directors, producers, and conductors tell them what to do. Know what you want and communicate how to get there.

Develop a close relationship with your sound and lighting technicians and expect them to be at rehearsals. They can make or break the flow of worship with what they do or don't do. Once again, do not forget to provide the necessary training to teach people what you want them to do.

REPRISE

One final word concerning building and leading a worship team is to have a spirit of hospitality. I believe one of the reasons we have had a successful worship ministry at Bethany is because our leadership has a hospitable spirit. People need to know that we love them. People are more inclined to participate in a ministry if they feel significant, loved, and challenged. I am on a journey on how to do this better every year. May God give you a similar heart for your people.

ten

WORSHIPING IN A TECHNOLOGICAL SOCIETY

HOW MUCH TECHNOLOGY should be incorporated into the worship service? Some tell us to catch up with culture; others tell us that the church is looking too much like the culture. I believe that we need to hear both voices. While technology does offer many possibilities, we need to consider the drawbacks as well.

Most of the structures we worship in require some technological enhancement such as sound, lighting, and computer systems. We cannot get around this reality. In order to be able to communicate appropriately, we must have good systems.

ACOUSTICAL CONCERNS

When I visited cathedrals in Prague, I was amazed at the architecture, the paintings, and the organs. I have attended many concerts in these cathedrals: Mozart's *Requiem*, The

History of Spanish Guitar recitals, and other performances highlighting well-known composers. To use amplification is unnecessary in these settings because the music and architecture go together. A rock concert in one of these buildings would be disastrous. The music should match the acoustical situation. So it will be in our own context.

Sound Systems

In my church, because of rebuilding and construction, we currently worship in the gym and use a sound system that is carefully designed to enhance our situation. Acoustical texturing along with dimensional design should concern every worship leader. A simple rule is that sound bounces off hard textures: rock, wood, cement, metal, and tile. Conversely, sound is absorbed with carpeting and texture that is padded. Most significantly, sound is absorbed by people.

One of the best investments you can make is hiring acoustical engineers to inspect your facility. They can take your facility through a computer process to determine how to design your system. Is this necessary? If communication is important to you, the answer is yes. I believe that people need to hear the gospel message. We should not be frugal in this area; we should spend the money to do the job right.

I have worshiped in hundreds of churches around the world where the sound systems have been inferior. I was listening to feedback and other distractions; what a squandering of resources. Many churches do not spend money on good sound systems. In fact, some people have better sound systems in their cars than we have in our churches. This is inexcusable. We should make communication of the gospel a priority.

Excellent sound systems are a must for dynamic worship services. Yet, sound systems are not magic; they cannot fix intonation or correct diction in the choir or match vowels in the praise team. Music comes from the platform, not the sound board. The sound system provides the necessary amplification.

A good sound system will enhance the worship environment and will eliminate distractions from the worship of Christ. It can help with the projection needed in most of our structures. Hearing a preacher communicate a sermon without feedback is crucial to the atmosphere of worship.

Training for Technicians

Along with an excellent sound system, you need training for your sound technicians. You need to have someone who knows your sound system train anyone who would desire to be a sound technician. Technicians need to know how the system works in the following areas: the sound board (what all the knobs and sliders stand for); the amps; the microphones (dynamic and condenser); the need for phantom power when using condenser mikes; troubleshooting (what to look for when feedback occurs); and what to listen for when working with a particular ensemble. Most importantly, find someone with musical ability who knows what to listen for musically in the ensemble.

Furthermore, find someone who understands his or her role. When I run a rehearsal, the technicians and I work together, but the ultimate responsibility is mine, not the technician's. I am employed at my church to oversee the worship services. Therefore, I do not hesitate to state what I want in a rehearsal or performance. I have a great relationship with our sound technicians and this above all else allows us to work together.

Purchasing Good Equipment

You should also acquire good equipment. This is a budget issue. Do not use leftover funds for the purchase of your equipment. Determine what you need, see what is out there, compare, and put a budget together. Go to your trustees and tell them why you need the equipment. When I came to Bethany in 1993, I wanted a MIDI compatible keyboard, with a built-in monitor, weighted eighty-eight keys, and modules for a variety of sounds. I shopped around for the lowest price and then brought a proposal to our trustees. In that I did my homework ahead of time, could articulate the purpose of such a proposal, and knew our budget, our trustees gave me the go-ahead to make the purchase. Today this system is still used as a primary keyboard in worship leading. With the built-in monitor strip, I have used this keyboard in rehearsals where I had no amplification available. With the weighted keys, it has been used by pianists at retreats and for other functions where no piano was available.

Buy the best microphones within your budget for your praise band, choir, and instrumentalists. Spend the money on a good piano—preferably a grand piano. Upright pianos usually lack a full sound in a sanctuary. Purchase good lapel microphones for your speakers. Spend money on a good CD player and cassette player. Purchase a drum set for your sanctuary if you are using contemporary music. The hassle of drummers setting up their own equipment is eliminated. They can come in and change the cymbals with their own if they prefer and bring a tuning key to make the necessary adjustments. The moment you make this decision, you will have drummers asking you if they can be on your praise team.

The most expensive purchase, other than a piano, will be an organ. You must decide how committed you are to this instrument. If you install a pipe organ, this will be the primary instrument in your sanctuary. There is nothing in the world like the sound of a pipe organ, but it may not be the wisest choice if you are going to use it on only one hymn each Sunday. It would be better to install an electronic organ with MIDI capability if you are blending your worship with choruses.

Please understand I am not saying that you must buy the most expensive equipment available. Rather, I am saying you should buy the best equipment you can afford. Prioritize the necessary purchases in your church budget to make your worship services beautiful.

MIDI TECHNOLOGY

MIDI simply means "Musical Instrument Digital Interface." With a MIDI compatible instrument, you can communicate data/information from a computer, a disk, or a module to a keyboard or other instrument. Do not be concerned if you do not understand all of this. Can you enjoy driving a car without being a mechanic? Of course. Likewise, you can enjoy the MIDI technology without understanding all the details.

I enjoy playing a Roland keyboard with a Korg module that contains endless possibilities. I literally have any instrument at my disposal: drums, guitars, Hammond organ, Fender Rhodes, brass, woodwinds, strings, and other sounds for different effects. I do not use all the sounds in this module, however. I have limited the sounds I use, which gives my worship leading a distinct sound. Nobody leads worship like me. This is not an arrogant statement; it is reality. I have my distinct personality, voice, and preference for sounds that I use on a weekly basis. The same is true for you. Use this technology to give you a distinct sound.

The benefits of having this technology are obvious. Yet, I must offer a warning. MIDI technology is being used in a destructive way: People are using it to replace musicians. If you are in a context in which you have a shortage of musicians, MIDI technology can be helpful. But remember what I said earlier: Musicians attract musicians. If you intentionally eliminate musicians, you will never have a worship team. Never use MIDI to replace musicians. I would rather hear just three people—a guitarist, a pianist, and a vocalist—lead worship than an orchestrated arrangement using only a keyboard. Remember that we have a biblical imperative to give the body of Christ a place to participate in the worship service (1 Cor. 14). Computers should never replace saints in the leading of the worship service when the saints are available to lead in worship!

COMPUTER TECHNOLOGY

Consider the community in which you minister. I live in Littleton, Colorado. Ten minutes from my church is the Denver Technical Center. Many of the people who attend my church are employed in the computer industry. When we added computer technology to our worship services, they appreciated it because they work and live in this kind of environment.

Computer technology, such as PowerPoint, can enhance singing, reading of Scripture, and the sermon. By using PowerPoint and a good video projector, you can have a sharper and cleaner projection system.

In my church, we use PowerPoint to put the words of the songs on the screen. This is especially helpful for the hymns. If you have mainly people who enjoy reading the music with the text, try projecting the words and the music. But if you have a situation like mine, where we have both literate musicians and people who are confused by music notation, try putting only the text on the screen and having hymnals available in the pew. By putting the hymn number next to the title of the song, those who like to read music can simply turn to the hymnal. Instead of getting up and saying, "Let's sing stanzas 1, 2, and 4," we have the stanzas/verses available. We put the hymn number next to the title for those who prefer using the hymnal. There are people who enjoy reading the music when they sing a hymn. But for everyone who does not read music, the words on the screen are helpful.

Make the words on the screen readable. You need to practice this in your sanctuary before a service. Go to the back of the sanctuary and see if you can read the words. Have a team representing different generations join you. Make it readable for them.

As with your sound technician, the person running PowerPoint needs to be at your rehearsals. Double-check that what is on the screen matches what you are doing. Remember, technology must enhance, not distract from, the worship of Christ.

One benefit of using PowerPoint for the reading of Scripture is that everyone can read the same translation together. If your church is like mine, we have people using multiple translations. This makes corporate reading impossible. It must have been easier many years ago when everyone was using the King James Bible. Likewise, traditions that use a prayerbook or something similar do not have this problem. But for most evangelical churches, having the Scripture verses on the screen allows for a smoother liturgy. The downside of using PowerPoint for this purpose is that you may discourage people from using their Bibles. The upside is that it is visitor friendly; even though visitors may not have a Bible with them when they come to church, they can still participate in the service.

A pastor who encourages people to take notes during the sermon can use PowerPoint effectively. I have always found it helpful when listening to a sermon to see as well as hear the main points. By having worshipers fill in blanks, a pastor can encourage active participation in the congregation. On the other hand, a pastor who is a master storyteller will have the attention of the people through spoken communication alone.

Generational distinctives should be made at this point. Baby Boomers really enjoy high-tech worship services—

especially if they have not grown up in a traditional church. They like PowerPoint. On the other hand, Gen Xers really like high-touch worship services. This postmodern generation likes a good story. PowerPoint is less helpful if you are going to be a storyteller.

You need to know whether technology is going to be an enhancement or a detraction in your worship service. In my church, we use technology, and most of our people really appreciate PowerPoint. But that might not be the situation in your church. Ask the Lord for wisdom and have people in your church give you honest feedback.

Lighting

I was recently watching a television program on which the guests on the show were discussing the greatest inventions that have contributed to rock music. One of the inventions discussed was the lightbulb. The reasoning was that you can have the greatest music, but if you cannot see the performer you cannot have a concert.

Certainly leading worship is more than leading a concert. Yet the issue of lighting is just as important. The best lighting is through the use of windows; there is nothing like natural light. If you do not have this available to you, good mechanical lighting should be installed. It is important for your musicians to be able to see the music. It is important that the people on the platform are not in the shadows. Everyone on the platform should be able to see and be seen.

Also, you should have good lighting on any symbols that you want to emphasize. If you have a cross in your sanctuary and want attention on it, good lighting is the answer. If you have banners and you want people to see the message or symbol, emphasize with good lighting.

If your congregation is using hymnals, they need to see their music. The same is true if they are reading from the Bible or taking sermon notes. But more important than the functional element of good lighting is that you as the worship leader should be able to *see* the body of Christ. Worship is about a redeemed people ascribing value to the King of kings, and lighting will bring out their beauty.

DEVELOPING A WEB SITE

Having a web site for your church can help promote your worship services. The communication possibilities of a phone book are great, but a web site will offer so much more. With a web site, you can introduce your community to your service times and to your staff. You can have a section on your theology of worship. People want to know what you believe; this will help them determine if they should join your congregation. You can also have some teaching about worship on your site. Furthermore, you can catalogue your teaching ministry with real audio.

The greatest challenge of having a web site is maintenance. It is beneficial to have one individual lead a team of people to keep your information updated. This person should be at the church every week to monitor the site and collate information.

A great benefit of having a web site is its nonthreatening way of introducing your community to your church. Instead of knocking on doors, which has overtones of the intrusive cults, you can inform your community about your church at their convenience. Instead of putting silly slogans on your marquee, you can advertise the web site address. You could also do a mailing and door hanger with your web site address printed on it. This is a great way to get the information out to your community.

E-MAIL AND THE WORSHIP COMMUNITY

I have all of the musicians at Bethany on e-mail. This is
a very effective way of communicating needed information
to people who help lead in worship. I have found that people check e-mail more frequently than answering machines.
Making numerous phone calls is time consuming and inef-
fective. It is easier to type one message and send it to everyone at once.

You could also have a daily, weekly, or quarterly devotional on worship to send to people in your church who
want worship teaching. Avoid messages that are too long.
E-mail is effective for quick information. If I receive e-
mails that are too long, I do not read them—depending
on the source. Use e-mail to communicate effectively. A
short psalm with a question for reflection or a short quote
on worship is ideal. For example, a slogan such as "God is
most glorified in us when we are most satisfied in Him" by
John Piper can be transformative in the worship of your
people.

FUTURE TECHNOLOGY

Begin the journey. Most technology is user friendly. Yet,
as much as I love to read, I hate reading technical manu-
als. Find people in your church who know the technology
and ask them to help you. Have them devote their time as
a ministry to share their expertise.

Involving other people will allow you to have balance.
Spending time on the Internet can become an addiction.
This is a waste of time. You need solitude, silence, and
reflection. As important as it is to keep current with technology, do not allow this to swallow up your time. There
is always a learning curve that is required to acquire new
technologies.

A decade ago, I made a decision to learn additional music theory and work on jazz piano voicings. This replaced learning new MIDI sounds and other programs that were available. I could spend hours playing with all of the new sounds instead of creating music. You also need to make a decision how much you are going to spend on technology. My theory about leadership is to find someone to do the job better than you and put them to work.

USING PEOPLE'S GIFTS

There are probably people in your church who are gifted and skilled in the areas of sound, lighting, and computer technology. Let them have a ministry. Empower them to use their talents for the glory of God. I have a technical team that includes sound and computer technicians for our worship services. I have a married couple that gives leadership to this ministry: The husband oversees our sound technology, and his wife, who is skilled in working with PowerPoint, runs that aspect of our services. Both of them come to rehearsals and begin the process of helping our Sunday worship services sound and look their best. Since they both know much more than I will ever know in these areas, I always consult them. We have a ministry together in worship.

I have finally settled in my soul that I will never know everything. I decided that I needed the body of Christ to support me if I was going to expand the worship ministries at Bethany. There are people who are waiting to be asked to help out. We tend to think that we are going to be begging people to get involved. Asking is the key: Ask the Father to provide the necessary help and ask people what they love to do and put them to work. The Bible tells us that this is how the church is to function.

Reprise

Technology can be a blessing to your worship ministry. Used with wisdom, it can enhance your worship services. Always use technology to bring the church together; never use it to isolate your people. Remember, the great commandment is to love God passionately and to love people compassionately. If you have this before you, there will be balance. I have found that the polemic voices that tell us to dive into technology without caution or to avoid technology at all costs are both extreme. Every good thing can be used for a bad purpose. Know the possibilities and the limitations of technology. Incorporate the good and avoid the bad. Most important, may God be glorified in your worship services. May the body of Christ be edified. And may your community know that God is in your midst. These should be the ultimate goals of the complete worship leader.

APPENDIX A

SUBDIVIDING

THE CHART BELOW lists various subdivisions. When working with time signatures, simply remember that the bottom number (or the right side) of the fraction tells you what the main unit is. The top part (or the left side) of the fraction tells you how many of the main units there are. For example, in 6/8 time, the main unit is an eighth note (right hand side of the fraction), and there are six eighth notes (6 is on the left hand side of the fraction).

In 4/4 time the main unit is the quarter note. A whole note=2 half notes=4 quarter notes=8 eighth notes=16 sixteenth notes. Counting this would be as follows:

For quarter notes—1 2 3 4 / 1 2 3 4/ etc.

For subdividing eighth notes—1 and 2 and 3 and 4 and/ 1 and 2 and 3 and 4 and/ etc.

For subdividing sixteenth notes—1 ee and uh 2 ee and uh 3 ee and uh 4 ee and uh/ etc.

In 3/4 time the main unit is the quarter note. A dotted half note=3 quarter notes=6 eighth notes=12 sixteenth notes. Counting this would be as follows:

For quarter notes—1 2 3/ 1 2 3/ etc.
For subdividing eighth notes—1 and 2 and 3 and/ 1 and 2 and 3 and/ etc.
For subdividing sixteenth notes—1 ee and uh 2 ee and uh 3 ee and uh/ etc.

In 6/8 time, the main unit is the eighth note. A dotted quarter note=3 eighth notes=6 sixteenth notes. In 6/8 time, it is infrequent that you will subdivide down to sixteenth notes for the very reason that most pieces written in 6/8 time are *scherzo* and have the feeling of a Strauss waltz. In other words, the tempo is usually fast. On the other hand, what you will find yourself doing is moving mathematically in the opposite direction (multiplying). You will normally place the emphasis on 1 and on 4 in 6/8 time to bring out the triplet feeling. For example: (1) 2 3 (4) 5 6/ (1) 2 3 (4) 5 6/ etc. Think of most 6/8 pieces in two. One . . . Two . . . / One . . . Two . . . / etc. Learning to subdivide can make all the difference in eradicating the tendency to speed up or slow down tempos.

APPENDIX B

TONGUE TWISTERS FOR ENUNCIATED SPEECH

1. Amos Ames, the amiable aeronaut, aided in an aerial enterprise at the age of eighty-eight.
2. Some shun sunshine. Do you shun sunshine?
3. Fine white wine vinegar with veal.
4. Bring a bit of buttered brown bran bread.
5. Geese cackle, cattle low, crows caw, cocks crow.
6. Eight gray geese in a green field grazing.
7. Six thistle sticks.
8. Lucy likes light literature.
9. A big black bug bit a big black bear.
10. Peter Prangle, the prickly prangly pear picker, picked three pecks of prickly prangly pears from the prickly prangly pear trees on the pleasant prairies.
11. Theophilus Thistle, the successful thistle sifter, in sifting a sieveful of unsifted thistles, thrust three thousand thistles through the thick of his thumb. Now if

Theophilus Thistle, the successful thistle sifter, in sifting a sieveful of unsifted thistles, thrust three thousand thistles through the thick of his thumb, see that thou in sifting a sieveful of unsifted thistles thrust not three thousand thistles through the thick of thy thumb. Success to the successful thistle sifter.[1]

APPENDIX C

REHEARSAL AND PERFORMANCE CONSIDERATIONS

1. Listen to various recordings of the piece you are practicing.
2. Arrive early at a performance. To be exactly on time is to be late. Always arrive in plenty of time to reduce stress and worry. This will also give you time to warm up and prepare for your performance.
3. Double-check that accompaniment tapes are cued up, music is all there, instruments are working, and that the circumstances have not been changed drastically from the rehearsal.
4. If you make a mistake, forget it and move on. You will be the only one who was aware of your mistake. You are best exposed with nonverbal gestures such as rolling the eyes, shrugging the shoulders, a discouraged look on your face.

5. Always say a simple "thank you" when people compliment you. Do not say you could have done better or other such comments. A true professional accepts a compliment. Eliminate the false humility. When people clap, acknowledge their appreciation with a smile or a bow.

6. Practice all transitions carefully. Avoid dead space (the time from one transition to another void of any sound). Fix it or it will destroy your performance.

7. Rehearse in a room with live acoustics. Tile, stone, and hard wood floors usually provide live acoustics. A heavily carpeted room will usually not be the ideal practice room. Exceptions would be in a band situation with a lot of amplified instruments. You would then modify a live acoustic situation to fit your circumstances.

8. Rest as long as you practice. Practicing is like weight lifting. If you keep lifting weights without taking a break, you are going to pull a muscle. If you are a brass player or a singer, you need to use common sense in protecting the embouchure or vocal chords. The old saying "No Pain, No Gain" is not appropriate for the musician. In my opinion, "No Pain, No Gain=No Brain." Take time to develop naturally. If you sing for four hours and then go and perform, you are going to feel the consequence.

9. Take good care of your health. If you are a singer, avoid caffeine, dairy products, and spicy foods before a performance. Caffeine dries out your vocal chords, and dairy products and the like produce unnecessary mucus. Also, acid reflux can inflame your larynx; this can lead to a nodule on your vocal chords. Drink room temperature water. Do not forget to get the necessary sleep prior to performance. Use common sense!!!

10. Practice with a tuner.

11. Practice near a piano.

12. Practice with a metronome.
13. Find a good accompanist.
14. Practice standing up and sitting down. Alternate during a session. To prevent boredom, go for brief walks during your sessions.
15. Practice mentally during resting periods. You do not always have to sing or play to rehearse.
16. Practice slowly. Never play a passage faster than you can play it correctly. Sloppiness is usually linked to impatience.
17. Practice consistently and frequently. It is better to practice fifteen minutes six times a week than to practice once a week for an hour and a half. There is accomplishment in routine.
18. There are three absolutely necessary capabilities every musician must possess in order to become a successful performer: the technical command to accomplish any desired musical effect; the good taste to use this technique musically and artistically; and the courage to accomplish both while in front of an audience. If nervousness on the stage is partly due to not being sure how well the performance will go, obviously any study or practice, previous to the performance, which will help to build accuracy and dependability, is very important. There is no more potent cure for stage fright than the knowledge that you can do it. And the only way you can know that you can do it is to know that you have done it—perhaps hundreds of times; the more often the better. That computer cannot be ignored. . . . Reduce the danger (of making mistakes) by that repetitious practice previously referred to, and reduce the novelty of appearing in public performance by appearing so often that the novelty wears off, and you will reduce the amount of adrenaline flowing into your bloodstream.[1]

19. If you are a pianist or a keyboard player, you must become familiar with "padding" (a jazz term for soft accompaniment, especially while somebody is speaking). The key is to think candlelight, not spotlight. The tempo should be rubato/strigendo in that, if you are playing in tempo, the speaker must think and therefore speak in the tempo that you are playing. This can be very distracting for somebody who is trying to communicate a very important message. You are to support, not compete with, the speaker. The key here is what you do not do.

NOTES

Introduction

1. The context suggests that worship was to be one of lifestyle. Jesus also encourages us to let our light shine before men in such a way that they may see our good works and glorify our Father in heaven (see Matt. 5:16).

2. Ralph Martin in his book on worship states: "We submit that no statement of the church's *raison d'etre* comes near to the heart of the biblical witness or the meaning of church history unless the worship of God is given top priority. The church exists for this reason above all else. It is called into being and continues to function in God's providence and grace to offer to the Father the sacrifice of praise and thanksgiving, and to celebrate the mighty acts of God in creation, redemption, and the final triumph of his kingdom in this world and beyond." Ralph Martin, *The Worship of God* (Grand Rapids: Eerdmans, 1982), 209.

Introduction to Part One

1. William H. Willimon, *Worship As Pastoral Care* (Nashville: Abingdon, 1979), 22.

2. For a detailed argument of the need for redemption to be the centerpiece of our worship, refer to chapter three of Robert Webber's *Worship Is a Verb* (Nashville: Abbott/ Martyn, 1992).

Chapter 1

1. For a wonderful sermon on the need for "wonder" in our worship services refer to Warren Wiersbe's sermon entitled "The Wonder of Worship"

(FW86–27) on the Moody Broadcasting Network Cassette Ministry (312-329-8010).

2. According to Gordon R. Lewis and Bruce A. Demarest in their work entitled *Integrative Theology*, general revelation refers to the disclosure of God in nature, in providential history, and in the moral law within the heart, whereby all persons at all times and places gain a rudimentary understanding of the Creator and his moral demands. Gordon R. Lewis and Bruce A. Demarest, *Integrative Theology* (Grand Rapids: Zondervan, 1987), 61.

3. David Peterson, *Engaging with God* (Grand Rapids: Eerdmans, 1992), 26.

4. Jesus summed up the first four articles of the decalogue in Matthew 22:37–40 when he stated, "You shall love the Lord your God with all your heart, and with all your soul, and with all your might. This is the great and foremost commandment" (NASB). If we will keep our passion directed toward the Creator, the prohibitions in the ten commandments will be fulfilled.

5. J. I. Packer, *Concise Theology* (Wheaton: Tyndale, 1993), xii.

6. Luci Shaw, *Polishing the Petoskey Stone* (Wheaton: Harold Shaw Publishers, 1990).

7. J. I. Packer states: "'In the beginning God created the heavens and earth' (Gen 1:1). He did it by fiat, without any preexisting material; his resolve that things should exist ('Let there be . . .') called them into being and formed them in order with an existence that depended on his will yet was distinct from his own. Father, Son, and Holy Spirit were involved together (Gen. 1:2; Pss. 33:6, 9; 148:5; John 1:1–3; Col. 1:15–16; Heb. 1:2; 11:3). Points to note are as follows: (a) The act of creation is mystery to us; there is more in it than we understand. We cannot create by fiat, and we do not know how God could. To say that he created 'out of nothing' is to confess the mystery, not explain it. In particular, we cannot conceive how dependent existence can be distinct existence, nor how angels and human beings in their dependent existence can be not robots but creatures capable of free decisions for which they are morally accountable to their Maker. Yet Scripture everywhere teaches us that this is the way it is. (b) Space and time are dimensions of the created order; God is not 'in' either; nor is he bound by either as we are. (c) As the world order is not self-created, so it is not self-sustaining, as God is. The stability of the universe depends on constant divine upholding; this is a specific ministry of the divine Son (Col. 1:17; Heb. 1:3), and without it every creature of every kind, ourselves included, would cease to be. As Paul told the Athenians, 'he himself gives all men life and breath and everything else. . . . In him we live and move and have our being' (Acts 17:25, 28). . . . Realizing our moment-by-moment dependence on God the Creator for our very existence makes it appropriate to live lives of devotion, commitment, gratitude, and loyalty toward him, and scandalous not to. Godliness starts here, with God the sovereign Creator as the first focus of our thoughts." J. I. Packer, *Concise Theology: A Guide to Historic Christian Beliefs* (Wheaton: Tyndale, 1993), 21–22.

8. It's imperative that our theology be Trinitarian as it pertains to the Creator. John 1:1, 3, 10 demonstrates the active role of the Son. In Genesis 1, we

clearly understand the Spirit of God *(ruach)* to be the source in which life has its inception.

9. Abraham Joshua Heschel, *The Sabbath* (New York: Harper Collins, 1951), 9. This is the best book on the topic of Sabbath that I have come across. Another is by Marva Dawn: *Keeping the Sabbath Wholly: Ceasing, Resting, Embracing, Feasting* (Grand Rapids: Eerdmans, 1989).

10. Also notice the following references that echo Genesis 1:26–27: Genesis 5:1; 9:6; 1 Corinthians 11:7; and James 3:9.

11. Graham Kendrick, *Learning to Worship As a Way of Life* (Minneapolis: Bethany House, 1984), 26.

CHAPTER 2

1. Formally defined, *special revelation* refers to the eternal God's disclosure of his redemptive purposes in the Near East (1) supremely through Jesus Christ's character, life, and conceptual teachings (in human words) confirmed by miraculous acts, and also (2) in various ways to prophetic and apostolic spokesmen whose teachings from God in human words were confirmed by their consistency with one another and by signs, wonders, and mighty acts. Gordon R. Lewis and Bruce A. Demarest, *Integrative Theology* (Grand Rapids: Zondervan, 1987), 110.

2. David Peterson, *Engaging with God: A Biblical Theology of Worship* (Grand Rapids: Eerdmans, 1992), 48.

3. Webber, *Worship Is a Verb*, 30.

4. J. B. Torrance, "The Place of Jesus Christ in Worship," in *Theological Foundations for Ministry*, ed. Ray S. Anderson (Grand Rapids: Eerdmans, 1979), 352.

5. Ibid.

6. Naida Hearn, *Jesus, Name Above All Names* (Scripture in Song, a div. of Integrity Music, Inc., 1974).

7. Ralph P. Martin, *The Worship of God: Some Theological, Pastoral, and Practical Reflections* (Grand Rapids: Eerdmans, 1982), 52–53.

8. It is interesting to note that Matthew in his gospel tells us that when the Magi came from the east to worship the Christ child, accompanied with their worship were gifts of gold, incense, and myrrh. The gifts are symbolic of the role the Messiah would play. The annotation at Genesis 37:25 in the NIV Study Bible states: "As a gift fit for a king, myrrh was brought to Jesus after his birth (Matt. 2:11) and applied to his body after his death (John 19:39–40), (p. 63). Clearly, the gifts were already celebrating the Christ events concerning redemption.

9. In an article entitled "Starved for Crumbs," Douglas Wilson states, "The cultural poverty within the church is considerable. Our idea of the cultural mandate is to ape whatever our disintegrating modern culture comes up with, after a respectable time lag of five to ten years. The only redeeming thing about our worldliness is that we carry it off badly. Anything the world can do, we can do afterwards and, hamstrung by our remaining biblical memories, worse. The faith, to paraphrase Paul Simon, 'ain't got no cultcha.' When the world comes up with thrasher bands, we want a thrasher band with John 3:16 somewhere in the liner notes." This article continues to criticize the church for taking its cues

from the impoverished culture around us. For the complete article see: Douglas Wilson, "Starved for Crumbs," in *Tabletalk* (December 1997), 58–59.

10. J. I. Packer, "The Word of God: Scripture as Revelation," in *The New Geneva Study Bible* (Nashville: Thomas Nelson, 1995), 141.

11. David Peterson states, "The Lord's Supper, which has its origin in Jesus' teaching at the Last Supper (c.f. Luke 22:29–30; 1 Cor. 11:26), is not itself to be regarded as the fulfilment of the Passover. In some respects, the Lord's Supper functions as a Christian substitute for the Passover, focusing on Jesus' death, rather than the exodus from Egypt, as the means by which God's people are saved and brought to share in the blessings of the inheritance promised to them." Peterson, *Engaging with God*, 121.

CHAPTER 3

1. As I mentioned in the first section of this work, theology becomes the grid in which we view this issue of worship. I clearly hold the position that we cannot possibly worship the Living God unless we are born again by the Spirit of God.

2. Gordon Fee, *Paul, the Spirit, and the People of God* (Peabody, Mass.: Hendrickson Publishers, 1996), 44.

3. I have found studying the Reformers and the Puritans much more enriching than devotional literature when it comes to developing a heart for the Living God. From the Reformational perspective, mercy and grace become rich terms that provide every incentive to worship the Father.

4. I know that by suggesting such a list I am putting myself at risk. Yet as I search the Scriptures, these kinds of ideas are clearly encouraged. For example, 2 Corinthians 13:5 tells us to "examine yourselves to see whether you are in the faith; test yourselves."

CHAPTER 4

1. Chapter 3, entitled "Kerygmatic Doxology," in *Themes and Variations for a Christian Doxology* deals with this idea of worship's being proclamation. Dr. Old goes into great detail as to why worship is essentially proclamation. Hughes Oliphant Old, *Themes and Variations for a Christian Doxology* (Grand Rapids: Eerdmans, 1992), 41–62.

2. For more information on the importance of keeping your marriage and family ahead of ministry as well as other related issues, see the article by Robb Redman, "Learning Strategies for the Long Haul," *Worship Leader* (January-February 1998): 26–29.

3. For detailed information on the various functions that a sermon has see: Ralph Martin, *The Worship of God* (Grand Rapids: Eerdmans, 1982), 101–23.

4. Eugene Peterson, *Subversive Spirituality* (Grand Rapids: Eerdmans, 1997), 178.

5. Rick Warren shares the importance of transparency and preaching through your weaknesses in an excellent tape, which can be found at the fol-

lowing source: The Leadership Summit 1997 tape series by Willow Creek Resources (1-800-727-3480).

Introduction to Part 3

1. Ronald Allen and Gordon Borror, *Worship: Rediscovering the Missing Jewel*, 27.

Chapter 6

1. Bennet Reimer, *A Philosophy of Music Education*, 2d ed. (Englewood Cliffs, N.J.: Prentice Hall, 1989), 25.
2. Allen and Borror, *Worship: Rediscovering the Missing Jewel*, 29–30.
3. Ibid., 97–98.
4. Philip Farkas, *The Art of Musicianship* (Bloomington, Ind.: Musical Publications, 1976), 29.
5. Reimer, *A Philosophy of Music Education*, 28.
6. Farkas, *The Art of Musicianship*, 13.
7. Ibid., 15.
8. Willi Apel, *Harvard Dictionary of Music* (Cambridge, Mass.: The Belknap Press of Harvard University Press, 1972), 668.
9. Farkas, *The Art of Musicianship*, 9.
10. Ibid., 9–10.
11. Ibid.
12. Ibid.
13. Ibid.
14. Ibid., 17.
15. Ibid., 18.
16. Ibid., 37.
17. I am grateful to Eugene Peterson for sharing this illustration at a *Discipleship Journal* conference in Colorado Springs.
18. Webber, *Worship Is a Verb*, 1.
19. Ibid., 25.

Chapter 7

1. There is a wonderful tape series entitled "Follow the Leader" by Eugene H. Peterson. These lectures address the issue of following Jesus. Peterson compares Jesus with Herod, Caiaphas, and Josephus. These tapes can be ordered from Regent Bookstore (1-800-663-8664) or through their web site (www.regentbookstore.com).
2. Joseph S. Carroll, *How to Worship Jesus Christ* (Chicago: Moody Press, 1984), 24–25.
3. Jack Hayford, *Worship His Majesty* (Milton Keynes, England: Word, 1987), 58.
4. Jack Taylor, *The Hallelujah Factor* (Nashville: Broadman, 1983), 16.
5. Barry Liesch, *The New Worship: Straight Talk on Music and the Church* (Grand Rapids: Baker, 1996), 23.

6. Allen and Borror, *Worship: Rediscovering the Missing Jewel*, 23.

7. Hughes Oliphant Old, *Themes and Variations for a Christian Doxology: Some Thoughts on the Theology of Worship* (Grand Rapids: Eerdmans, 1992), 17, 24.

8. Peterson, *Engaging with God*, 28.

9. Ralph P. Martin, *The Worship of God: Some Theological, Pastoral, and Practical Reflections* (Grand Rapids: Eerdmans, 1982), 6.

Chapter 8

1. Allen and Borror, *Worship: Rediscovering the Missing Jewel*, 16.

2. Jack Hayford makes the assertion in his book *Worship His Majesty*, that worship is not only *by* the people of God but also *for* the people of God. Worship is the means by which the Holy Spirit brings about the Kingdom of God amongst the body of Christ.

3. One of the best books dealing with a theology of hospitality as it pertains to corporate worship is: Patrick R. Keifert, *Welcoming the Stranger: A Public Theology of Worship and Evangelism* (Minneapolis: Fortress Press, 1992).

4. An excellent resource for training in this area is: John Maxwell, *Ushers and Greeters* (Injoy). This three-part tape series and notebook can be ordered by calling 1-800-333-6506.

5. Martin, *The Worship of God*, 13.

6. Jack Hayford, John Killinger, and Howard Stevenson, *Mastering Worship* (Portland, Oreg.: Multnomah, 1990), 98, 106–7.

7. For more information on song selection for the best participatory response see part one in: Liesch, *The New Worship*.

8. The following resources have been very helpful to me in planning a flow in worship services: Liesch, *The New Worship*; Hayford, Killinger, and Stevenson, *Mastering Worship*; Bob Sorge, *Exploring Worship: A Practical Guide to Praise and Worship* (Canandaigua, N.Y.: Oasis House, 1987); Doug Murren, *How to Design Contemporary Worship Services* (Ventura, Calif.: Gospel Light, 1994). This last resource is a videotape designed to help traditional churches make the transition to contemporary worship.

9. Allen and Borror, *Worship: Rediscovering the Missing Jewel*, 23–24.

10. Chuck Kraft, "Beneath Our Words: The Determining Factor in Our Worship Is the Nature of our Relationship with God," *Worship Leader* (Sept./Oct. 1996): 17.

Appendix B

1. Jim Custer and Bob Hoose, *The Little Book of Theater Games* (Kansas City, Mo.: Lillenas Publishing Co., 1997), 81.

Appendix C

1. Farkas, *The Art of Musicianship*, 48–49.

BIBLIOGRAPHY

Allen, Ronald, and Gordon Borror. *Worship: Rediscovering the Missing Jewel.* Three Sisters, Oreg.: Questar Publishers, 1982.

Apel, Willi. *Harvard Dictionary of Music.* Cambridge, Mass.: The Belknap Press of Harvard University Press, 1972.

Bruser, Madeline. *The Art of Practicing: A Guide to Making Music From the Heart.* New York: Bell Tower, 1977.

Carroll, Joseph S. *How to Worship Jesus Christ.* Chicago: Moody Press, 1984.

Copland, Aaron. *What to Listen For in Music.* New York: Mentor Books, 1939.

Custer, Jim, and Bob Hoose. *The Little Book of Theater Games.* Kansas City, Mo.: Lillenas, 1997.

Dawn, Marva J. *Keeping the Sabbath Wholly: Ceasing, Resting, Embracing, Feasting.* Grand Rapids: Eerdmans, 1989.

Farkas, Philip. *The Art of Musicianship.* Bloomington, Ind.: Musical Publications, 1976.

Fee, Gordon D. *Paul, the Spirit and the People of God.* Peabody, Mass.: Hendrickson Publishers, 1996.

Foster, Richard. *Celebration of Discipline: The Path to Spiritual Growth.* San Francisco: Harper and Row, 1978.

_____. *Prayer: Finding the Heart's True Home.* San Francisco: HarperCollins, 1992.

Hayford, Jack. *Worship His Majesty*. Dallas: Word, 1987.

Hayford, Jack, John Killinger, and Howard Stevenson. *Mastering Worship*. Three Sisters, Oreg.: Questar Publishers, 1990.

Heschel, Abraham Joshua. *The Sabbath*. New York: Farrar, Strauss, & Giroux, 1951.

Hostadter, Albert, and Richard Kuhns. *Philosophies of Art and Beauty: Selected Readings in Aesthetics from Plato to Heidegger*. Chicago: The University of Chicago Press, 1964.

Keifert, Patrick R. *Welcoming the Stranger: A Public Theology of Worship and Evangelism*. Minneapolis: Fortress, 1992.

Kendrick, Graham. *Learning to Worship as a Way of Life*. Minneapolis: Bethany House, 1985.

Kraft, Chuck. "Beneath Our Words: The Determining Factor in Our Worship Is the Nature of Our Relationship with God." *Worship Leader* (Sept-Oct, 1996): 17.

Langer, Susanne K. *Philosophy in a New Key: A Study in the Symbolism of Reason, Rite, and Art*. Cambridge, Mass.: Harvard University Press, 1942.

Lewis, Gordon, and Bruce Demarest. *Integrative Theology*. Grand Rapids: Zondervan, 1987.

Liesch, Barry. *People in the Presence of God: Models and Directions for Worship*. Grand Rapids: Zondervan, 1988.

_____. *The New Worship: Straight Talk on Music and the Church*. Grand Rapids: Baker Books, 1996.

Martin, Ralph P. *The Worship of God: Some Theological, Pastoral and Practical Reflections*. Grand Rapids: Eerdmans, 1982.

McGinnis, Alan Loy. *Bringing Out the Best in People*. Minneapolis: Augsburg, 1985.

Meyers, Kenneth A. *All God's Children and Blue Suede Shoes: Christians and Popular Culture*. Wheaton: Crossway Books, 1989.

Morganthaler, Sally. "The Song of the People." *Worship Leader* (March/April 1997): 14, 27.

_____. *Worship Evangelism*. Grand Rapids: Zondervan, 1995.

Nouwen, Henri. *In the Name of Jesus: Reflections on Christian Leadership*. New York: Crossroad, 1989.

Old, Hughes O. *Leading in Prayer: A Workbook for Worship*. Grand Rapids: Eerdmans, 1995.

_____. *Themes and Variations for a Christian Doxology*. Grand Rapids: Eerdmans, 1992.

Packer, J. I. *Concise Theology: A Guide to Historic Christian Beliefs*. Wheaton: Tyndale, 1993.

Peterson, David. *Engaging With God: A Biblical Theology of Worship*. Grand Rapids: Eerdmans, 1992.

Peterson, Eugene. *Subversive Spirituality*. Grand Rapids: Eerdmans, 1997.

_____. *Take and Read: Spiritual Reading: An Annotated List*. Grand Rapids: Eerdmans, 1996.

Reimer, Bennet. *A Philosophy of Music Education*. Englewood Cliffs, N.J.: Prentice Hall, 1989.

Saliers, Don E. *Worship Come to Its Senses*. Nashville: Abingdon Press, 1996.

Schula, Don, and Ken Blanchard. *Everyone's a Coach*. New York: Harper Business, 1995.

Shaw, Luci. *Polishing the Petoskey Stone*. Wheaton: Harold Shaw, 1990.

Sorge, Bob. *Exploring Worship: A Practical Guide to Praise and Worship*. New York: Oasis House, 1987.

Tan, Siang-Yang, and Douglas Gregg. *Disciplines of the Holy Spirit: How to Connect to the Spirit's Power and Presence*. Grand Rapids: Zondervan, 1997.

Taylor, Jack R. *The Hallelujah Factor*. Nashville: Broadman Press, 1983.

Torrance, J.B. "The Place of Jesus Christ in Worship," in *Theological Foundations for Ministry*, ed. Ray S. Anderson. (Grand Rapids: Eerdmans, 1979), 348–369.

Towns, Elmer. *Putting an End to Worship Wars*. Nashville: Broadman and Holman Publishers, 1997.

Veith, Gene Edward. *State of the Arts: From Bezalel to Mapplethorpe*. Wheaton: Crossway Books, 1991.

Wardle, Terry. *Exalt Him! Designing Dynamic Worship Services*. rev. ed. Camp Hill, Penn.: Christian Publications, 1992.

Webber, Robert E., ed. *The Complete Library of Christian Worship, 7 volumes*. Nashville: Star Song, 1993–94.

_____. *Worship Is a Verb*, 2d ed. Nashville: Abbot-Martyn, 1992.

White, James F. *A Brief History of Christian Worship*. Nashville: Abingdon, 1993.

_____. *Protestant Worship: Traditions in Transition*. Louisville, Ky.: Westminister/John Knox, 1989.

Willard, Dallas. *In Search of Guidance: Developing a Conversational Relationship with God*. San Francisco: Harper/Zondervan, 1993.

_____. *The Spirit of the Disciplines: Understanding How God Changes Lives*. San Francisco: HarperCollins, 1988.

Willimon, William H. *Worship as Pastoral Care*. Nashville: Abingdon, 1979.

Wright, Timothy. *A Community of Joy: How to Create Contemporary Worship*. Nashville: Abingdon, 1994.

KEVIN J. NAVARRO has been leading worship in the local church and with para-church ministries for eighteen years. Prior to becoming a Christian, Kevin was a nightclub musician.

He attended the University of Northern Colorado where he received his Bachelor of Music and Bachelor of Music Education. Kevin also graduated from Denver Seminary with a Master of Divinity and from Fuller Theological Seminary with a Doctorate of Ministry. This blend of musical and theological education allows Kevin to teach about worship as an artist, theologian, and pastor. In the May/June 2000 issue of *Worship Leader*, Robb Redman featured Kevin as an example of the importance of pursuing continuing education as a worship leader.

Furthermore, Kevin J. Navarro was an international director for the Continental Singers. He has led the Continentals through thirty-seven countries including: the Netherlands, Germany, Denmark, Norway, Sweden, Finland, Estonia, Romania, Yugoslavia, Hungary, England, Wales, Austria, Switzerland, Belgium, New Zealand, Australia, Singapore, Malaysia, the Philippines, Japan, Puerto Rico, Columbia, Mexico, and Venezuela. This experience has been invaluable in understanding the body of Christ from an international perspective, especially as it pertains to styles of worship, art forms, and liturgies.

Kevin J. Navarro has been an adjudicator for the Christian Artist Seminar (Estes Park, Colorado) in the vocal and instrumental categories. He has also taught on the topic of worship for a number of retreats and conferences.

Currently, Kevin J. Navarro lives with his wife and four boys in Littleton, Colorado, where he is a pastor and worship leader at Bethany Evangelical Free church.